IN ASSOCIATION WITH

✕ SQA

HODDER GIBSON

Model Papers

WITH ANSWERS

FREE
audio files to accompany this title can be accessed at
www.hoddergibson.co.uk
• Click on the blue 'Updates and Extras' box.
• Look for the 'SQA Papers Audio Files' heading and click the 'Browse' button beneath.
• You will then find the files listed by language and year.

PLUS: Official SQA 2014 & 2015 Past Papers With Answers

National 5
German

Model Papers, 2014 & 2015 Exams

HODDER GIBSON
AN HACHETTE UK COMPANY

This book contains the official SQA 2014 and 2015 Exams for National 5 German, with associated SQA approved answers modified from the official marking instructions that accompany the paper.

In addition the book contains model papers, together with answers, plus study skills advice. These papers, some of which may include a limited number of previously published SQA questions, have been specially commissioned by Hodder Gibson, and have been written by experienced senior teachers and examiners in line with the new National 5 syllabus and assessment outlines, Spring 2013. This is not SQA material but has been devised to provide further practice for National 5 examinations in 2014 and beyond.

Hodder Gibson is grateful to the copyright holders, as credited on the final page of the Answer Section, for permission to use their material. Every effort has been made to trace the copyright holders and to obtain their permission for the use of copyright material. Hodder Gibson will be happy to receive information allowing us to rectify any error or omission in future editions.

Hachette UK's policy is to use papers that are natural, renewable and recyclable products and made from wood grown in sustainable forests. The logging and manufacturing processes are expected to conform to the environmental regulations of the country of origin.

Orders: please contact Bookpoint Ltd, 130 Park Drive, Milton Park, Abingdon, Oxon OX14 4SE. Telephone: (44) 01235 827720. Fax: (44) 01235 400454. Lines are open 9.00–5.00, Monday to Saturday, with a 24-hour message answering service. Visit our website at www.hoddereducation.co.uk. Hodder Gibson can be contacted direct on: Tel: 0141 848 1609; Fax: 0141 889 6315; email: hoddergibson@hodder.co.uk

This collection first published in 2015 by
Hodder Gibson, an imprint of Hodder Education,
An Hachette UK Company
2a Christie Street
Paisley PA1 1NB

Typeset by Aptara, Inc.

Printed in the UK

A catalogue record for this title is available from the British Library

ISBN: 978-1-4718-6059-1

3 2 1

2016 2015

Introduction
Study Skills – what you need to know to pass exams!

Pause for thought

Many students might skip quickly through a page like this. After all, we all know how to revise. Do you really though?

Think about this:

"IF YOU ALWAYS DO WHAT YOU ALWAYS DO, YOU WILL ALWAYS GET WHAT YOU HAVE ALWAYS GOT."

Do you like the grades you get? Do you want to do better? If you get full marks in your assessment, then that's great! Change nothing! This section is just to help you get that little bit better than you already are.

There are two main parts to the advice on offer here. The first part highlights fairly obvious things but which are also very important. The second part makes suggestions about revision that you might not have thought about but which WILL help you.

Part 1

DOH! It's so obvious but …

Start revising in good time

Don't leave it until the last minute – this will make you panic.

Make a revision timetable that sets out work time AND play time.

Sleep and eat!

Obvious really, and very helpful. Avoid arguments or stressful things too – even games that wind you up. You need to be fit, awake and focused!

Know your place!

Make sure you know exactly **WHEN and WHERE** your exams are.

Know your enemy!

Make sure you know what to expect in the exam.

How is the paper structured?

How much time is there for each question?

What types of question are involved?

Which topics seem to come up time and time again?

Which topics are your strongest and which are your weakest?

Are all topics compulsory or are there choices?

Learn by DOING!

There is no substitute for past papers and practice papers – they are simply essential! Tackling this collection of papers and answers is exactly the right thing to be doing as your exams approach.

Part 2

People learn in different ways. Some like low light, some bright. Some like early morning, some like evening / night. Some prefer warm, some prefer cold. But everyone uses their BRAIN and the brain works when it is active. Passive learning – sitting gazing at notes – is the most INEFFICIENT way to learn anything. Below you will find tips and ideas for making your revision more effective and maybe even more enjoyable. What follows gets your brain active, and active learning works!

Activity 1 – Stop and review

Step 1

When you have done no more than 5 minutes of revision reading STOP!

Step 2

Write a heading in your own words which sums up the topic you have been revising.

Step 3

Write a summary of what you have revised in no more than two sentences. Don't fool yourself by saying, "I know it, but I cannot put it into words". That just means you don't know it well enough. If you cannot write your summary, revise that section again, knowing that you must write a summary at the end of it. Many of you will have notebooks full of blue/black ink writing. Many of the pages will not be especially attractive or memorable so try to liven them up a bit with colour as you are reviewing and rewriting. **This is a great memory aid, and memory is the most important thing.**

Activity 2 – Use technology!

Why should everything be written down? Have you thought about "mental" maps, diagrams, cartoons and colour to help you learn? And rather than write down notes, why not record your revision material?

What about having a text message revision session with friends? Keep in touch with them to find out how and what they are revising and share ideas and questions.

Why not make a video diary where you tell the camera what you are doing, what you think you have learned and what you still have to do? No one has to see or hear it, but the process of having to organise your thoughts in a formal way to explain something is a very important learning practice.

Be sure to make use of electronic files. You could begin to summarise your class notes. Your typing might be slow, but it will get faster and the typed notes will be easier to read than the scribbles in your class notes. Try to add different fonts and colours to make your work stand out. You can easily Google relevant pictures, cartoons and diagrams which you can copy and paste to make your work more attractive and **MEMORABLE**.

Activity 3 – This is it. Do this and you will know lots!

Step 1

In this task you must be very honest with yourself! Find the SQA syllabus for your subject (www.sqa.org.uk). Look at how it is broken down into main topics called MANDATORY knowledge. That means stuff you MUST know.

Step 2

BEFORE you do ANY revision on this topic, write a list of everything that you already know about the subject. It might be quite a long list but you only need to write it once. It shows you all the information that is already in your long-term memory so you know what parts you do not need to revise!

Step 3

Pick a chapter or section from your book or revision notes. Choose a fairly large section or a whole chapter to get the most out of this activity.

With a buddy, use Skype, Facetime, Twitter or any other communication you have, to play the game "If this is the answer, what is the question?". For example, if you are revising Geography and the answer you provide is "meander", your buddy would have to make up a question like "What is the word that describes a feature of a river where it flows slowly and bends often from side to side?".

Make up 10 "answers" based on the content of the chapter or section you are using. Give this to your buddy to solve while you solve theirs.

Step 4

Construct a wordsearch of at least 10 × 10 squares. You can make it as big as you like but keep it realistic. Work together with a group of friends. Many apps allow you to make wordsearch puzzles online. The words and phrases can go in any direction and phrases can be split. Your puzzle must only contain facts linked to the topic you are revising. Your task is to find 10 bits of information to hide in your puzzle, but you must not repeat information that you used in Step 3. DO NOT show where the words are. Fill up empty squares with random letters. Remember to keep a note of where your answers are hidden but do not show your friends. When you have a complete puzzle, exchange it with a friend to solve each other's puzzle.

Step 5

Now make up 10 questions (not "answers" this time) based on the same chapter used in the previous two tasks. Again, you must find NEW information that you have not yet used. Now it's getting hard to find that new information! Again, give your questions to a friend to answer.

Step 6

As you have been doing the puzzles, your brain has been actively searching for new information. Now write a NEW LIST that contains only the new information you have discovered when doing the puzzles. Your new list is the one to look at repeatedly for short bursts over the next few days. Try to remember more and more of it without looking at it. After a few days, you should be able to add words from your second list to your first list as you increase the information in your long-term memory.

FINALLY! Be inspired...

Make a list of different revision ideas and beside each one write **THINGS I HAVE** tried, **THINGS I WILL** try and **THINGS I MIGHT** try. Don't be scared of trying something new.

And remember – "FAIL TO PREPARE AND PREPARE TO FAIL!"

National 5 German

You have chosen to add a national qualification in German to your education. Congratulations – it is one of the most sought-after foreign languages for business and trade in Scotland and in Europe.

What can National 5 do for you?

National 5 German is a course which has been developed by teachers and educational leaders to meet the requirements for Modern Foreign Languages in the 21st century.

The aim of the course is to give you confidence in understanding (reading and listening) and using (speaking and writing) German in the following contexts:

- Society (Family and friends, Lifestyle, Media, Global languages, Citizenship)
- Learning (Learning in context, Education)
- Employability (Jobs, Work and CVs)
- Culture (Planning a trip, Other countries, Celebrating a special event, German literature, German films and TV)

What does the Course Assessment look like?

Reading and Writing

You will have 1 hour and 30 minutes for both parts of this paper. This question paper will have 50 marks in total – 50% of the overall course marks.

The Reading paper

The reading part of this paper will have 30 marks – 10 marks for each text.

You will read three German texts of between 150 and 200 words each. Questions on the text are set in English, and you must respond in English. These questions will ask for specific details about the text, but there will also be an **overall purpose question**.

You may use a dictionary in this paper.

> ### What is the "overall purpose"?
>
> Whenever you read a text (or listen to a text) in any language, you should be aware that texts are produced for a reason and/or a certain audience. This could be to advertise a product, to promote a place of interest, to express concern about a situation, to invite somebody to an event, to give an opinion about a matter – to name but a few. This should sound familiar to you from your English classes.

You will have to show understanding of the overall purpose of a text in your course assessment in Reading and in Listening by answering a supported question (multiple choice) correctly.

The Writing paper

You will produce one written text, a job application in German, in response to a stimulus supported by six bullet points which you must address. See them as a checklist of information that you will have to provide in your response.

Four of the bullet points are predictable but two of them are less predictable as they vary from year to year.

The text you produce must take the form of an e-mail and should be between 120 to 150 words in length.

You may use a dictionary in this paper.

Listening

The Listening paper

This question paper will have 20 marks – 20% of the total mark.

You will listen to one monologue (approximately one and a half minutes long) and one short dialogue (approximately two to two and a half minutes long) in German. You will be asked questions in English and must respond in English.

The monologue is worth 8 marks and it is necessary for you to understand the overall purpose of the spoken text (see *What is the "overall purpose"?*, below left).

The dialogue is worth 12 marks and it has a topical link to the monologue.

You may not use a dictionary in this paper.

Speaking

The speaking assessment will be carried out in your school by your German teacher, who will be able to help you to prepare for it well in advance. It will be recorded and marked by your teacher.

The speaking assessment has two parts:

1 **A presentation in German on a topic of your choice,** such as:
   - Meine Familie und ich
   - Meine Freizeit und meine Freunde
   - Meine Heimatstadt
   - Meine Schule und meine Schulkarriere
   - Meine Zukunftspläne
   - Mein Arbeitspraktikum
   - Mein Lieblingsfilm
   - Mein Lieblingsbuch

The presentation should be approximately two to three minutes long, you may use notes (not sentences) and/or visual support such as a PowerPoint presentation, a picture, a photograph, an item, etc.

2 A discussion with your teacher in German

Your teacher will ask you additional questions on your presentation or may ask questions which relate to a topic derived from your presentation. The discussion should be approximately three to five minutes long.

The total mark for your speaking exam at National 5 is 30. Five out of these 30 marks will only be granted if the language you use in the conversation is natural and spontaneous.

What can you do to help you have a successful National 5 German exam?

Top Tip: Do not panic!

As soon as the exam timetable is published, ask your teacher for the exact date of the German exam (usually April/May time) and mark the date and time in your diary – or on your mobile phone.

Remember that your Speaking exam will be done before your Reading and Writing and Listening exams. Take this into account when you plan your revision.

Reading tips

Before you read the German texts:

- read the title/headline and ask yourself what you already know about the topic.
- look at any pictures as they support the contents of a text.
- check if the text comes with a glossary to save yourself time looking up words in the dictionary.

While you are reading the German texts:

- focus on your reading – be an active reader!
- try to figure out the main idea(s) of the text(s).
- access the meaning of a word by
  - checking the context/sentence the word is in.
  - checking if the word is similar to English (German and English have many cognates or near cognates – which are words that look and/ or sound similar or even the same); many German and English words begin with the same letter or even the same two letters.
  - checking whether or not the text comes with a glossary.
  - using the dictionary.

After you have read the text and before you start answering the questions:

- read the comprehension questions carefully.
- if necessary, underline the question word to highlight exactly what kind of answer is required.
- check the tense form of the English question to make sure you use the same tense form in your answer.
- make sure that your answer has sufficient detail – compare it with the marks you can get for each answer.

Most importantly – make sure your English answers make sense and your English expression is of a good standard.

After you have answered the questions:

- allow yourself time to go over your answers.

Writing tips

Before you sit your writing exam:

- plan the exam carefully by exploring the four predictable bullet points:
  - Make sure you know the proper conventions for your piece of writing and practise them.
  - Make a note of some vocabulary which you will need to address these bullet points and learn it. Choose five verbs, five adjectives and five nouns, for example.
  - Remember what you have practised in class when covering the topic areas you are writing about.
  - Produce a draft and show it to your teacher before the exam.

While you are sitting your writing exam:

- read the stimulus very carefully and identify exactly what the job is that you are going to apply for. Use the dictionary for help, if necessary, and remember that jobs in German have male and female forms.
- read the two bullet points which are less predictable. Remember what you have learned in class about the topics they address.
- avoid writing very long sentences as you may lose control of structure and word order. However, try to include connectors such as und/aber/oder/denn and also some which change the word order such as weil/obwohl/dass.
- try to use different tense forms where possible, e.g. "Ich habe im letzten Jahr ein Arbeitspraktikum gemacht."/ "Ich werde das Abitur machen und Deutsch studieren."

- where possible, include opinions using German expressions such as "Ich denke, dass..."/ "Ich bin der Meinung, dass..."/"Ich finde..."/"Meiner Meinung nach..."
- try not to translate from English as you will be tempted to apply the English sentence structure rather than the German one – focus on the correct position of the verb in the German sentence and remember the rules of German sentence structure.
- limit yourself to 20 to 25 words per bullet point and make sure you address them all.
- focus on capitalisation of nouns and correct verb endings to achieve a high level of accuracy.

After you have finished your writing exam:
- leave yourself enough time at the end to proofread your e-mail text.
- check that you have addressed all six bullet points.
- check your verb endings and tense forms, your adjective endings and capitalisation of nouns.
- if in doubt, use the dictionary for support.

Listening tips

Top Tip: Learn your vocabulary regularly and revise systematically before the exam. Only those who recognise words will be able to understand the meaning of a spoken sentence.

Before you sit your listening exam:
- revise vocabulary, especially verbs in their different tense forms, quantifiers (viel, wenig, die meisten), numbers and dates. Read vocabulary out loud so that you recognise acoustically what you see in front of you.
- read the title/the introduction to the listening item and ask yourself what your experience with the topic is and what you know about this topic.
- remember the close relationship between the English and the German language where many words sound very similar and use this to your benefit in listening. However, beware: "Schinken" is not "chicken"!
- read the English questions very carefully – you have one minute to study them – and underline the question words or any others which you feel might be of importance.
- remember that the questions are in chronological sequence – the answer to question (c) must be between the answers to (b) and (d) in the recording.

While you are sitting your listening exam:
- remember that both items (monologue and dialogue) will be played three times so it is not necessary to answer any questions during the first playing.
- write your answers neatly and clearly on your question paper. If you correct your answer, make sure the marker will be able to recognise your final answer.
- if you don't understand a word which you believe to be an element of an answer – do not panic! Trust your instincts and your natural connection to German as a speaker of English and see if you can guess the meaning.
- be guided by the number of marks allocated to each question. They will tell you how much information is expected in your answer.

After your listening exam:
- go over your answers. Make sure your English expression is as good as possible to convey meaning clearly.
- make sure you have crossed out any draft answers leaving the final answer for the marker to see.

Speaking tips

Top tips:
- **Start preparing for your speaking exam in plenty of time. Practise speaking regularly as practice makes perfect.**
- **Remember that your teacher will conduct the exam and that he/she will want to help you to succeed. Trust him/her.**

Before your speaking exam:
- choose a topic that you really like and have something to say about for your presentation.
- develop a piece of writing for your presentation which has a clear structure. Show this work to your teacher.
- ask your teacher to read aloud and record this text for you on your mobile phone, iPod or any other media device so that you can listen to it many times before the exam.
- turn the sentences of that text into notes. (A note is a short phrase which does not contain a verb.)
- practise your presentation by listening to the recording and reading your notes, then try it without the recording by your teacher.
- try to figure out what kind of questions your teacher might ask you in the discussion. These questions will be linked to the topic you have presented.

For example:

If you have done a presentation on your favourite film, your teacher might ask questions such as:

- "Siehst du gern fern oder gehst du lieber ins Kino?"
- "Was findest du besser – DVDs zu Hause oder einen Kinofilm mit Freunden?"
- "Hast du einen Lieblingsschauspieler/eine Lieblings-schauspielerin? Warum findest du ihn/sie gut?"
- "Welche Filme siehst du gern?"
- "Welche Fernsehsendungen siehst du gern?"

Make sure you revise and learn conventions on expressing an opinion in German, e.g. "Ich finde ...", "Ich bin der Meinung, dass...", "Meiner Meinung nach..." etc.

You should also revise and learn conventions on how to sustain a conversation – especially when you have difficulties understanding a question, e.g. "Ich habe das nicht verstanden. Bitte wiederholen Sie die Frage."/ "Ich bin nicht sicher, was das auf Deutsch/Englisch heißt."/ "Sprechen Sie bitte langsamer."

During your speaking exam:

- concentrate on your notes in your presentation. You are entitled to use them – do not do without.

- look up from your notes, keep eye contact and speak loudly and clearly to show you are confident – and to ensure a good quality of recording!

- do not panic if you are stuck – try to recover by remembering what you have worked out for your presentation.

- listen carefully to your teacher's questions and remember that you can always "steal" vocabulary from the question to make your answer.

- try to avoid very long sentences as you might lose control over the sentence structure. However, try to use connectors such as und/aber/oder/denn and also weil.

- ask for help (in German) when you need it. This will not necessarily result in a lower mark as it shows your ability to use German for clarification purposes.

After your speaking exam:

- ask your teacher if it is possible to listen to your recording and get some feedback on your performance.

- you might want to use your National 5 speaking exam as a basis for your Higher speaking exam – so keep your notes if you are thinking about taking Higher German.

In your National 5 Course Assessment, the formula to success is a sound knowledge of the level of German required, teamwork in class and with your teacher, and confidence in yourself and the skills your teacher has helped you to develop. Most importantly though, enjoy the course and the experience. Deutsch ist mega cool!

Good luck!

Remember that the rewards for passing National 5 German are well worth it! Your pass will help you get the future you want for yourself. In the exam, be confident in your own ability. If you're not sure how to answer a question, trust your instincts and just give it a go anyway. Keep calm and don't panic! GOOD LUCK!

Model Paper 1

Whilst this Model Paper has been specially commissioned by Hodder Gibson for use as practice for the National 5 exams, the key reference documents remain the SQA Specimen Paper 2013 and the SQA Past Papers 2014 and 2015.

HODDER
GIBSON
LEARN MORE

National Qualifications
MODEL PAPER 1

German
Reading

Duration — 1 hour and 30 minutes

Total marks — 30

READING — 30 marks

Read all THREE texts and attempt ALL questions.

MARKS | DO NOT WRITE IN THIS MARGIN

READING — 30 marks

Text 1

You are reading a German youth magazine and have found this interesting article about a British student in Hamburg.

Eine Britin in Hamburg

Gemma ist 20 Jahre alt und kommt aus Großbritannien. Sie studiert britisches und europäisches Recht an der Universität von Sheffield. Seit zwei Monaten lebt und arbeitet sie in Hamburg, einer großen Stadt in Norddeutschland.

„Ich habe in der Schule Deutsch gelernt und diese Sprache relativ einfach gefunden. Als ich dann mein Abitur in der Tasche hatte, bin ich mit meinen Freunden mit dem Zug durch ganz Europa gefahren. Am besten hat es uns in Deutschland gefallen — tolle Leute, toller Service und echt gutes Essen!

Meine Universität hat allen Studenten ein Jahr im europäischen Ausland empfohlen und da war es für mich klar, dass ich nach Deutschland gehen möchte. Ich mache im Moment ein Arbeitspraktikum in Hamburg und bin von der Stadt an der Elbe total begeistert.

Hamburg hat mehr als zwei Millionen Einwohner; es gibt hier viele Parks und sehr viel Wasser, sodass man gar nicht denkt, dass man in einer Großstadt lebt. Meine Arbeitskollegen sind echt hilfsbereit und freundlich; wir gehen am Wochenende ins Kino oder in einen der vielen Klubs auf der Reeperbahn.

Ich bin verliebt in Hamburg!"

Questions   MARKS

(a) How long has Gemma been living and working in Hamburg?   1

_____

(b) Why did Gemma and her friends like Germany best? Mention **three**
     things.   3

_____

_____

_____

(c) What does Gemma say about Hamburg? Mention **three** things.   3

_____

_____

_____

(d) What is her relationship with her work colleagues like? Give a reason for
     your answer.   2

_____

_____

(e) Overall, what impression does the text give about Gemma's Hamburg
     experience? Tick the correct box.   1

The text gives an overall positive view of Gemma's work experience in Hamburg.	
The text gives an overall negative view of Gemma's work experience in Hamburg.	

Total marks 10

MARKS | DO NOT WRITE IN THIS MARGIN

Text 2

You then read about a British-German couple in Berlin.

Brian und Sabine — verliebt in Berlin

In der heutigen Zeit ist es nicht ungewöhnlich, dass die Liebe Ländergrenzen überschreitet. Die Zahl der bi-nationalen Paare in Deutschland nimmt zu; jedes vierte in Deutschland geborene Kind hat ein nicht-deutsches Elternteil.

Brian und Sabine Sadler gehören zu dieser Gruppe, sie wohnen beide in Berlin, aber Brians Heimatstadt ist Glasgow. Vor fünf Jahren haben sich Brian und Sabine bei einer Umweltkonferenz in Hannover kennen gelernt. Brian war dort als Repräsentant einer schottischen Energiefirma und Sabine hat an der Rezeption im Hotel gearbeitet. Es war Liebe auf den ersten Blick!

Brian hat Sabine oft in Deutschland besucht und sie ist auch nach Schottland gekommen, um Brians Familie und sein Heimatland besser kennen zu lernen.

Weil Sabine einen guten Job in Berlin bekommen hat, haben die beiden entschieden, dass sie in der deutschen Hauptstadt wohnen werden. Brian musste sein Deutsch verbessern und selbst auf Jobsuche gehen. Er hat schnell Arbeit gefunden, denn er hat einen Universitätsabschluss und spricht Englisch und Deutsch.

Vermisst er Schottland? „Ja, ein bisschen schon — aber Glasgow ist nur 90 Minuten mit dem Flugzeug entfernt, das ist kein Problem für mich."

Questions   MARKS

(a) What evidence is there that love nowadays is becoming more and more international? Mention any **one** thing.   **1**

_____

_____

(b) When and where did Brian and Sabine meet?   **2**

_____

_____

(c) Why did Sabine visit Scotland?   **2**

_____

_____

(d) What did Brian have to do before moving to Berlin?   **2**

_____

_____

(e) Why was it easy for him to find a job?   **2**

_____

_____

(f) Think about what you have read. How does Brian feel about his new life in Berlin? Tick the correct box.   **1**

Brian is missing Scotland a lot and wants to move back to Glasgow.	
Brian is happy in Berlin and finds it easy to visit Glasgow if he wants to.	

Total marks 10

Text 3

On the hobby and leisure page of the youth magazine, you find this article about dogs as pets.

Wie ist das Leben mit einem Hund?

Thomas hat von seinen Eltern zu Weihnachten einen Hund bekommen — einen Boxerwelpen mit dem Namen „Bonzo". Wie gefällt Thomas das Leben mit seinem vierbeinigen Freund?

„Zuerst habe ich mich total gefreut, dass ich Bonzo bekommen habe. Als Einzelkind kann das Leben ganz schön langweilig sein. Aber dann habe ich gemerkt, dass ein Hund auch sehr viel Verantwortung bedeutet. Man muss dreimal täglich mit ihm Gassi gehen (einen Spaziergang machen), man muss mit ihm zum Tierarzt und vor allem muss man einen Hund richtig trainieren, damit es mit den Nachbarn keine Probleme gibt. Das war ganz schön schwierig für mich, denn ich hatte vorher noch nie einen Hund oder ein anderes Haustier. Um Fehler zu vermeiden, habe ich mir ein Buch zum Thema Hundeerziehung gekauft. Im Internet habe ich auch noch eine Hundeschule in unserer Nähe gefunden, zu der wir einmal in der Woche gehen.

Am besten finde ich, dass Bonzo mich fit hält. Wir laufen durch den Wald oder durch den Park, ich kann ohne Probleme mit ihm joggen und das hilft mir bei meinem Training im Fußballverein. Ich denke, dass ein Hund besser ist als jedes Fitnessstudio und dass man als Hundebesitzer super viel Spaß hat."

(a) Why was Thomas delighted about his Christmas present? **1**

_____

(b) What did he soon realise? **1**

_____

(c) According to Thomas, what must you do when you have a dog? Mention **three** things. **3**

_____

_____

_____

(d) Where did Thomas find help with his new responsibility? Mention **two** things. **2**

_____

_____

(e) According to Thomas, what is best about having Bonzo? **1**

_____

Text 3 Questions (continued)

(f) Overall, does Thomas recommend a dog as a pet? Give a reason for your answer.

2

_____

_____

Total marks 10

[END OF READING PAPER]

[BLANK PAGE]

National Qualifications
MODEL PAPER 1

German
Writing

Duration — 1 hour and 30 minutes

Total marks — 20

WRITING — 20 marks

Use **blue** or **black** ink.

You may use a German dictionary.

MARKS

WRITING — 20 marks

You are preparing an application for the job advertised below and you write an e-mail **in German** to the company.

Teilzeitjobs mit Perspektive

Der private Post-und Paketedienst „Merkur" in Berlin sucht Mitarbeiter auf Teilzeitbasis.

Wir bieten Ihnen:

- einen sicheren Arbeitsplatz
- einen sehr guten Stundenlohn
- sehr gute Sozialleistungen
- innerbetriebliche Weiterbildung
- sehr gute Karrierechancen

Sie helfen in unserer Firma beim Beladen und Entladen von Containern. Außerdem sortieren Sie Pakete und Postsendungen. Sie arbeiten auch im Büro und im Paketlager.

Sie sollten fleißig, pünktlich und ordentlich sein. Sie sollten am Computer arbeiten können und sehr gute Deutsch-und Englischkenntnisse haben.

Haben Sie Interesse? Sehr gut — bitte bewerben Sie sich per E-Mail: merkurpakete@netzmix.de

---

To help you to write your e-mail, you have been given the following checklist of information to give about yourself and to ask about the job. You must include all of these points:

- Personal details (name, age, where you live)
- School/college/education experience until now
- Skills/interests you have which make you right for the job
- Related work experience
- What kind of office work you are able to do
- Why you would like to work in Berlin

Use all of the above to help you write the e-mail in **German**, which should be approximately 120–150 words. You may use a **German** dictionary.

MARKS

ANSWER SPACE

ANSWER SPACE (continued)

ANSWER SPACE (continued)

ANSWER SPACE (continued)

[END OF WRITING PAPER]

MARKS DO NOT WRITE IN THIS MARGIN

ADDITIONAL SPACE FOR ANSWERS

ADDITIONAL SPACE FOR ANSWERS

National Qualifications MODEL PAPER 1

German Listening

Duration — 25 minutes

Total marks — 20

You will hear two items in German. **Before you hear each item, you will have one minute to study the question.** You will hear each item three times, with an interval of one minute between playings. You will then have time to answer the questions about it before hearing the next item.

Write your answers clearly, **in English**, in the spaces provided.

You may take notes as you are listening to the German.

Use **blue** or **black** ink.

You may NOT use a German dictionary.

MARKS

Item 1

You are attending a pupil conference at a German language institute. Participants are asked to introduce themselves. You are listening to Anna, a German teenager.

(a) How old is Anna?   1

_____

(b) Why is she in St Andrews at the moment?   1

_____

(c) What does she say about Bremen, her home town in Germany? Write any **two** things.   2

_____

_____

(d) What does Anna do in her spare time? Write **one** thing.   1

_____

(e) What kind of person is Anna? Give **two** details.   1

_____

_____

(f) Who are Tom and Jerry?   1

_____

(g) What impression does Anna give about her time in Scotland? Tick the correct box.   1

Anna is homesick and is not enjoying her stay in St Andrews.	
Anna is enjoying her stay in St Andrews and would like to return as a student.	
Anna cannot see herself coming back to Scotland again.	

Total marks   8

MARKS | DO NOT WRITE IN THIS MARGIN

Item 2

Paul spent a year as an exchange student in Edinburgh. He is being interviewed for a local radio station in Germany.

(a) What does Paul say about Edinburgh? Mention any **two** things.   2

_____

_____

(b) Which of these statements are correct? Tick **two** boxes.   2

Paul's host family lives on the outskirts in the west of Edinburgh.	
Paul shared a room in the house.	
Paul had a TV and a computer in his room.	
Paul had no contact with his German family and friends.	

(c) Paul talks about school in Scotland. What did he find different from school in Germany? Mention any **three** things.   3

_____

_____

_____

(d) Where did Paul go twice a week?   1

_____

(e) What did he and his host family do in St Andrews? Mention **two** things.   2

_____

_____

(f) Give any **two** reasons why Paul thinks that a year abroad is a good idea.   2

_____

_____

Total marks 12

[END OF LISTENING PAPER]

[BLANK PAGE]

National Qualifications
MODEL PAPER 1

German
Listening Transcript

Duration — 25 minutes (approx)

This paper must not be seen by any candidates.

The material overleaf is provided for use in an emergency only (e.g. the recording or equipment proving faulty) or where permission has been given in advance by SQA for the material to be read to candidates with additional support needs. The material must be read exactly as printed.

HODDER GIBSON
LEARN MORE

Transcript – National 5

> **Instructions to reader(s):**
>
> For each item, read the English **once**, then read the German **three times**, with an interval of 1 minute between the three readings. On completion of the third reading, pause for the length of time indicated in brackets after the item, to allow the candidates to write their answers.
>
> Where special arrangements have been agreed in advance to allow the reading of the material, those sections marked **(f)** should be read by a female speaker and those marked **(m)** by a male; those sections marked **(t)** should be read by the teacher.

(t)   Item number one.

You are attending a pupil conference at a German language institute. Participants are asked to introduce themselves. You are listening to Anna, a German teenager.

You now have one minute to study the questions.

(f)   Ich heiße Anna und ich bin 16 Jahre alt. Mein Geburtstag ist am dritten Januar. Im Moment bin ich als Austauschschülerin in St Andrews, das ist eine kleine Stadt an der Ostküste von Schottland.

Ich komme aus Bremen — das ist eine große Stadt im Westen von Deutschland. Bremen ist bekannt für Fußball und die Bremer Stadtmusikanten. Bremen ist meine Heimatstadt, ich wohne sehr gern dort.

Ich habe eine Schwester, die Susanne heißt und achtzehn Jahre alt ist. In meiner Freizeit tanze ich sehr gern — einmal in der Woche gehe ich zum Ballettunterricht. Ich esse sehr gern Obst — am liebsten Weintrauben und Orangen. Ich habe Angst vor Spinnen und Schlangen.

Ich denke, dass ich ein freundlicher und lustiger Mensch bin. Manchmal kann ich ein bisschen launisch sein und leider bin ich nicht immer pünktlich.

Zu Hause in Bremen habe ich zwei Haustiere — meine beiden Hunde Tom und Jerry. Ich vermisse sie – aber in zwei Monaten bin ich wieder zu Hause.

Schottland gefällt mir sehr gut, obwohl das Wetter oft schlecht ist und es relativ viel regnet. Aber die Leute hier sind super toll, freundlich und hilfsbereit. Ich würde sehr gern als Studentin nach St Andrews zurückkommen.

(2 minutes)

(t)　**Item number two.**

Paul spent a year as an exchange student in Edinburgh. He is being interviewed for a local radio station in Germany.

You now have one minute to study the questions.

(m/f)　**Hallo Paul, herzlich willkommen zurück in Deutschland. Wie hat es dir in Edinburgh gefallen?**

(m)　Edinburgh ist eine tolle Stadt mit einer interessanten Geschichte und vielen Sehenswürdigkeiten. Es hat mir sehr gut in Schottland gefallen, obwohl das Wetter in Deutschland besser ist.

(m/f)　**Wo hast du gewohnt?**

(m)　Ich habe bei einer schottischen Gastfamilie gewohnt. Das Haus war am Stadtrand von Edinburgh im Westen der Stadt in der Nähe vom Flughafen. Ich hatte mein eigenes Zimmer und sogar einen Fernseher und Computer, sodass ich im Internet surfen und Kontakt mit meiner Familie und meinen Freunden in Deutschland haben konnte.

(m/f)　**Und wie war es in der Schule?**

(m)　Naja, es war schon total anders als in Deutschland. In Schottland gibt es Gesamtschulen und hier in Deutschland gehe ich auf ein Gymnasium. Außerdem beginnt die Schule in Schottland um neun Uhr und nicht um acht Uhr. Man isst Mittag in der Schule und hat Unterricht bis halb vier — ein langer Tag!

(m/f)　**Hast du schnell Freunde gefunden?**

(m)　Ja, das war kein Problem für mich. Ich bin zweimal pro Woche zum Rugbytraining gegangen und habe dort neue Freunde kennen gelernt. Einmal sind wir dann in das nationale Rugbystadion Murrayfield gegangen — das war ein besonderes Erlebnis.

(m/f)　**Und was hast du noch in Schottland gesehen?**

(m)　Meine Gastfamilie ist mit mir nach Glasgow gefahren. Außerdem waren wir im Hochland in Fort William und auf der Insel Skye. Am besten hat mir St Andrews gefallen — das ist eine kleine Stadt an der Ostküste mit der ältesten Universität von Schottland. Wir sind dort am Strand spazieren gegangen und haben Golf gespielt.

(m/f)　**Denkst du, dass es gut ist, ein Jahr im Ausland zu verbringen?**

(m)　Ja, auf jeden Fall. Man lernt eine neue Lebensart und eine neue Kultur kennen. Außerdem wird man selbstbewusster und unabhängiger. Mein Englisch hat sich natürlich auch verbessert. Und ich habe zwei neue Sportarten gelernt — Rugby und Golf. Hier in Deutschland spielt man ja lieber Fußball.

(m/f)　**Danke, Paul, dass du zu uns ins Studio gekommen bist.**

(2 minutes)

(t)　**End of test.**
Now look over your answers.

[END OF TRANSCRIPT]

[BLANK PAGE]

Model Paper 2

Whilst this Model Paper has been specially commissioned by Hodder Gibson for use as practice for the National 5 exams, the key reference documents remain the SQA Specimen Paper 2013 and the SQA Past Papers 2014 and 2015.

National Qualifications
MODEL PAPER 2

German
Reading

Duration — 1 hour and 30 minutes

Total marks — 30

READING — 30 marks

Read all THREE texts and attempt ALL questions.

MARKS

READING — 30 marks

Text 1

You are looking through a German teenage magazine and you come across an article about the effects of kissing.

Küssen ist gesund

Mehr als 80 Prozent der Deutschen sind der Meinung, dass Küssen entspannend ist und glücklich macht. Außerdem haben deutsche und amerikanische Wissenschafter festgestellt, dass Küssen sehr gesund ist.

Bei einem intensiven Kuss verbrennt man etwa 12 Kalorien und mehr als 30 Muskeln im Gesicht und am Hals sind aktiv. Diese Art von „Gymnastik" beugt Falten vor, schützt die Zähne vor Karies, senkt Stresshormone und stärkt das Immunsystem. Ein Kuss ist somit mehr als Zärtlichkeit — ein Kuss ist gesund für Körper und Seele!

Wie reagieren deutsche Teenager auf diese wissenschaftlichen Ergebnisse?

Tina (16) aus Bremen:

„Ich bin seit sechs Monaten mit meinem Freund Mark zusammen. Küssen ist sehr wichtig für unsere Beziehung — und ich finde es toll, dass es ein bisschen wie Sport ist!"

Thomas (17) aus Dresden:

„Ich finde Küssen super schön, denn man zeigt einem Menschen, dass er etwas Besonderes ist. Wenn das mein Immunsystem stärkt — umso besser!"

Susanne (15) aus Potsdam:

„Wir haben in der Schule ein Projekt zum International Tag des Kusses am 6. Juli gemacht. In diesem Projekt haben wir sehr viel über das Küssen gelesen, gehört und im Internet recherchiert. Das war total spannend — sowas lernt man normalerweise in der Schule nicht."

MARKS

Questions

(a) What do more than 80% of Germans believe? Mention any **one** thing.   1

_____

(b) According to the passage, what have the scientists found to be the positive effects of kissing? Mention any **three** things.   3

_____

_____

_____

(c) What does Tina compare kissing with?   1

_____

(d) According to Thomas, what does he show by giving somebody a kiss?   1

_____

(e) When did Susanne's school do a project on kissing?   1

_____

(f) Mention any **two** activities that Susanne did during the project.   2

_____

_____

(g) Think about why this article may have been published in the magazine.

Tick the most appropriate reason for publication.   1

The author of the article wants to entertain the readers.	
The author of the article wants to highlight that kissing has positive effects on people's health.	
The author wants to encourage young people to talk about health issues.	

Total marks   10

MARKS

Text 2

You read an interesting article about a special event for young people in Berlin.

Die YOU in Berlin

YOU — das ist die wichtigste Ausstellung zum Thema Jugendkultur in Deutschland. Jedes Jahr im Sommer kommen mehr als 100.000 Jugendliche nach Berlin, um in den Messehallen am Sommergarten mehr über die Themen Musik, Sport und Lebensstil von jungen Menschen in Deutschland zu erfahren.

Das Programm der YOU ist spannend und abwechslungsreich. Man kann nationale und internationale Musikstars erleben, mit DJs eine Party feiern oder selbst sein Talent auf der Bühne präsentieren. Außerdem gibt es viele Sportarten, die man ausprobieren kann — allein oder im Team.

Es gibt aber nicht nur Freizeit- und Sportaktivitäten auf der YOU. Es geht in der Ausstellung auch um die Themen Bildung, Karriere und Zukunft. Firmen und Berufsschulen helfen mit Informationen und Tipps zum Start ins Berufsleben. Jugendliche können Fragen stellen und herausfinden, welcher Beruf der richtige ist.

Das Motto der YOU ist „Mitmachen-Anfassen-Ausprobieren". Jugendliche sollen aktiv ihr Leben gestalten und selbst Initiative zeigen.

Wenn man die YOU besuchen möchte, kann man mit der S-Bahn oder der U-Bahn fahren. Es gibt auch sehr viele Parkplätze für Autos und Motorräder. Tickets für den Besuch bekommt man online unter www.you.de.

Questions

MARKS | DO NOT WRITE IN THIS MARGIN

(a) Complete the sentences with the correct English words.

YOU — this is the most _____ exhibition with a focus

on _____ in Germany.   **2**

(b) Why is the number 100.000 mentioned in the text?   **1**

_____

(c) According to the second paragraph, the programme of the event is exciting and varied. Give any **two** examples of activities available for young people attending this event mentioned in this paragraph.   **2**

_____

_____

(d) Apart from leisure and sport activities, what other aspects of life does YOU offer help with for young people? Mention any **two** things.   **2**

_____

_____

(e) Explain what the motto of this event encourages young people to do. Mention any **one** thing.   **1**

_____

(f) What can you do via the website www.you.de?   **1**

_____

(g) Overall, why has this article been published in the teenage magazine? Tick the most appropriate reason for publication.   **1**

The article wants to encourage young people to visit this exhibition.	
The article shows young people what they can do in the future.	
The article promotes Berlin as a city for young people.	

Total marks 10

MARKS | DO NOT WRITE IN THIS MARGIN

Text 3

You then read an article about young Germans and their opinion on dream jobs.

Traumberuf — Realität oder Fiktion?

Wir haben Jugendliche gefragt, ob es einen Traumberuf gibt oder nicht.

Bernd (18 Jahre, Auszubildender bei der Post):

„Ich arbeite als Paketzusteller bei der Post. Ich stehe sehr gern früh auf und habe keine Probleme gute Arbeit zu leisten. Außerdem fahre ich sehr gern Auto. Am besten finde ich, dass ich Menschen eine Freude machen kann – besonders zu Weihnachten, denn in vielen Paketen sind Geschenke von Familie und Freunden. Ich habe meinen Traumberuf gefunden."

Martina (17 Jahre, Krankenschwester in der Ausbildung)

„Als ich klein war, wollte ich sehr gern Tierärztin werden. Ich habe dann in der Schule ein Arbeitspraktikum bei einem Tierarzt gemacht. Die Arbeit hat mir nicht gefallen, sodass ich mich für eine Ausbildung als Krankenschwester entschieden habe. Der Alltag im Krankenhaus ist sehr stressig, ich habe sehr viele Patienten und oft keine Zeit. Am besten gefällt mir die Kinderstation — vielleicht studiere ich später Medizin und werde Kinderärztin."

Britta (16 Jahre, Schülerin)

„Ich denke, dass es keinen Traumberuf gibt, denn jeder Beruf hat gute und nicht so gute Seiten. Man muss sich fragen, ob der Beruf interessant ist und es genug Arbeitsplätze gibt. Der Arbeitsmarkt ist sehr wichtig — ich möchte auf keinen Fall arbeitslos sein."

(a) What personal qualities does Bernd bring to his job? Mention any **two** things.

2

(b) What does he like best about his job? Mention **one** thing.

1

(c) Explain why Martina changed her opinion about becoming a vet.

2

Text 3 Questions (continued)

(d) Why does Martina find her daily routine in the hospital stressful? Mention **two** things.

2

_____

_____

(e) Britta takes a practical approach to choosing a future career. What does she find important? Mention any **two** things.

2

_____

_____

(f) Think about what you have read. Which of the three young people has found their dream job? Tick the correct box.

1

Bernd	
Martina	
Britta	

Total marks 10

[END OF READING PAPER]

[BLANK PAGE]

National Qualifications
MODEL PAPER 2

German
Writing

Duration — 1 hour and 30 minutes

Total marks — 20

WRITING — 20 marks

Use **blue** or **black** ink.

You may use a German dictionary.

HODDER
GIBSON
LEARN MORE

WRITING — 20 marks

You are preparing an application for the job advertised below and you write an e-mail **in German** to the company.

Telefonieren Sie gern? Haben Sie Freude an Kommunikation?

Dann bewerben Sie sich bei uns!

Vieltelefonierer gesucht!

Wir sind eine Hamburger Firma und organisieren Konzerte und Massenveranstaltungen. Wir suchen einen Mitarbeiter/eine Mitarbeiterin auf Teilzeitbasis für einen Monat (Juni).

Dieser Job ist ideal für Studenten, die freundlich und höflich am Telefon sind. Sie sollten eine klare Aussprache haben, sichere Deutschkenntnisse sowie Kenntnisse in anderen europäischen Sprachen.

Ihr Aufgabenbereich:

- Kundenberatung
- Organisation und Koordination von Terminen
- Telefoninterviews
- Arbeit mit dem firminternen Computersystem und MS Office

Was bieten wir Ihnen?

- eine freundliche Arbeitsatmosphäre
- ein professionelles Team
- €12 pro Stunde
- Sozialversicherung

Haben Sie Interesse? Super! Bitte bewerben Sie sich auf der Webseite unserer Firma: www.makino.eu

---

To help you to write your e-mail, you have been given the following checklist of information to give about yourself and to ask about the job. You must include all of these points:

- Personal details (name, age, where you live)
- School/college/education experience until now
- Skills/interests you have which make you right for the job
- Related work experience
- Your view on modern communication technology/networking
- What you hope to learn during your time with the Hamburg firm

Use all of the above to help you write the e-mail **in German**, which should be approximately 120–150 words. You may use a **German** dictionary.

MARKS

ANSWER SPACE

ANSWER SPACE (continued)

MARKS | DO NOT WRITE IN THIS MARGIN

ANSWER SPACE (continued)

ANSWER SPACE (continued)

[END OF WRITING PAPER]

ADDITIONAL SPACE FOR ANSWERS

Page seven

ADDITIONAL SPACE FOR ANSWERS

National Qualifications
MODEL PAPER 2

German
Listening

Duration — 25 minutes

Total marks — 20

You will hear two items in German. **Before you hear each item, you will have one minute to study the question.** You will hear each item three times, with an interval of one minute between playings. You will then have time to answer the questions about it before hearing the next item.

Write your answers clearly, **in English**, in the spaces provided.

You may take notes as you are listening to the German.

Use **blue** or **black** ink.

You may NOT use a German dictionary.

MARKS | DO NOT WRITE IN THIS MARGIN

Item 1

Simone, a 16-year-old German girl, talks about her view on modern technology.

(a) According to Simone, which group of people like netbooks? **1**

_____

(b) Which advantages of netbooks does Simone mention? **2**

_____

_____

(c) Since when has Simone had a mobile phone? **1**

_____

(d) What does Simone do with her mobile phone? Mention any **three** things. **3**

_____

_____

_____

(e) What is Simone's overall view on modern technology? Tick the correct box. **1**

Simone thinks that modern technology is not really important.	
Simone's mobile phone is important to her and she loves to meet her friends online.	
Simone's mobile phone is important to her but she prefers to meet her friends face-to-face rather than online.	

Total marks 8

MARKS | DO NOT WRITE IN THIS MARGIN

Item 2

You are staying with your exchange partner Christian and his family in Germany. You are listening to a conversation between Christian and his mother about the time he spends with modern media.

(a) How much time did Christian spend on the computer last night?　　**1**

_____

(b) What did he do on the computer last night? Mention any **three** things.　　**3**

_____

_____

_____

(c) Why does Christian not like to watch TV at the moment? Mention any **two** things.　　**2**

_____

_____

(d) Which of these statements is correct? Tick **two** boxes.　　**2**

Christian likes the cinema a lot.	
Christian prefers to watch DVDs at home.	
Christian thinks that sitting at home is not boring.	
Christian does not have many friends at school.	

(e) Why does Christian not miss his friends when he is at home? Mention any **two** things.　　**2**

_____

_____

(f) Why does Christian like the idea of going to town by bus? Mention **two** things.　　**2**

_____

_____

Total marks　**12**

[END OF LISTENING PAPER]

[BLANK PAGE]

National Qualifications
MODEL PAPER 2

German
Listening Transcript

Duration — 25 minutes (approx)

This paper must not be seen by any candidates.

The material overleaf is provided for use in an emergency only (e.g. the recording or equipment proving faulty) or where permission has been given in advance by SQA for the material to be read to candidates with additional support needs. The material must be read exactly as printed.

Transcript – National 5

> **Instructions to reader(s):**
>
> For each item, read the English **once**, then read the German **three times**, with an interval of 1 minute between the three readings. On completion of the third reading, pause for the length of time indicated in brackets after the item, to allow the candidates to write their answers.
>
> Where special arrangements have been agreed in advance to allow the reading of the material, those sections marked **(f)** should be read by a female speaker and those marked **(m)** by a male; those sections marked **(t)** should be read by the teacher.

(t) Item number one.

Simone, a 16-year-old German girl, talks about her view on modern technology.

You now have one minute to study the questions.

(f) Für junge Leute ist es ganz normal einen Computer oder einen Laptop zu haben. Die meisten Jugendlichen gehen nicht ohne Handy aus dem Haus und Studenten arbeiten sehr gerne mit Netbooks, weil sie praktisch und flexibel sind.

Ich habe seit meinem zehnten Lebensjahr ein Handy und finde das super. Ein Handy ist mehr als ein Telefon. Man kann nicht nur telefonieren und texten, man kann auch im Internet surfen, E-mails checken, Fotos machen und Videos aufnehmen. Die meisten Handys haben auch eine soziale Netzwerk-Funktion, sodass man sehr schnell Zugang zu Facebook und Twitter hat.

Aber ich bin auch der Meinung, dass es nicht gut ist, wenn man zu viel Zeit mit Facebook und am Computer verbringt. Das Internet ist eine virtuelle Welt; sie hat nichts mit der Realität zu tun.

Ich treffe lieber meine Freunde im Café oder im Kino statt auf Facebook. Der persönliche Kontakt ist mir wichtig. Auch wenn man mehr als zweihundert Facebook-Freunde hat, kann man trotzdem im Internet sehr alleine und einsam sein.

(2 minutes)

(t)   Item number two.

You are staying with your exchange partner Christian and his family in Germany. You are listening to a conversation between Christian and his mother about the time he spends with modern media.

You now have one minute to study the questions.

(f)   **Christian, sag mal, wie lange hast du gestern Abend am Computer gesessen?**

(m)   Nicht so lange. Vielleicht zwei Stunden. Ich habe meine E-mails gecheckt und war auf Facebook. Dann habe ich noch Musik heruntergeladen und ein paar Videos auf Youtube gesehen.

(f)   **Warum siehst du Videos im Internet? Du hast doch einen Fernseher in deinem Zimmer!**

(m)   Das ist richtig — aber das Fernsehprogramm ist im Moment eine Katastrophe! Es gibt nur total langweilige Talentshows oder Seifenopern — nichts für mich.

(f)   **Warum gehst du denn nicht ins Kino?**

(m)   Ja, mal sehen. Ich sitze lieber auf dem Sofa zu Hause und sehe eine DVD. Ich kann mein Pyjama tragen und die DVD stoppen, wenn ich zur Toilette muss oder etwas zu trinken aus der Küche holen will. Es ist einfach bequemer und praktischer zu Hause.

(f)   **Mensch, Christian, du kannst nicht nur zu Hause sitzen. Das ist doch langweilig, oder nicht?**

(m)   Das ist gar nicht langweilig! Ich habe mein Handy und kann damit meine Freunde kontakten. Wir texten oder wir chatten auf Facebook. Und meine Freunde sehe ich jeden Tag in der Schule.

(f)   **Schule ist nicht Freizeit. Du solltest mal etwas mit deinen Freunden unternehmen. Warum fahrt ihr nicht mal mit dem Bus in die Stadt?**

(m)   Das ist eine gute Idee. Im Bus auf dem Weg in die Stadt kann ich dann mit meinem Handy Musik hören oder mein neues Nintendo DS Spiel testen!

(f)   **Christian!!!!!**

(2 minutes)

(t)   **End of test.**
   Now look over your answers.

Note: In the recording on the audio file, 'DVD' has been given the English pronunciation in error. Students should be aware that native language interference should be avoided in unit and course assessments.

[END OF TRANSCRIPT]

[BLANK PAGE]

Model Paper 3

Whilst this Model Paper has been specially commissioned by Hodder Gibson for use as practice for the National 5 exams, the key reference documents remain the SQA Specimen Paper 2013 and the SQA Past Papers 2014 and 2015.

HODDER
GIBSON
LEARN MORE

National Qualifications
MODEL PAPER 3

German Reading

Duration — 1 hour and 30 minutes

Total marks — 30

READING — 30 marks

Read all THREE texts and attempt ALL questions.

READING – 30 marks

Text 1

You are surfing the internet and have come across a German website. This interesting article about an American student in Germany attracts your attention.

Studieren in Deutschland – mega cool!

Ich heiße Toby und komme aus den USA. Seit zwei Jahren studiere ich Politik an der Universität Rostock im Nordosten von Deutschland. Meine Eltern waren nicht begeistert, dass ich zum Studium nach Europa gehen wollte. Aber ich habe es gemacht – und es war die beste Entscheidung meines Lebens.

Die Atmosphäre an meiner Universität ist sehr locker. Man kann seine Kurse selbst wählen und auch den Stundenplan selbst zusammenstellen. Wenn ich Probleme habe, gehe ich zu meinem Tutor oder zur Studentenvertretung. Das Studium ist nicht so teuer wie in den USA und mit einem deutschen Abschluss habe ich sehr gute Chancen für meine Karriere.

Zum Glück habe ich in der Schule in Amerika Deutsch gelernt. Aber seit ich hier in Deutschland studiere, spreche ich die Sprache fließend und problemlos. In den letzten zwei Jahren bin ich unabhängiger und weltoffener geworden. Am Wochenende und in den Ferien bin ich durch Deutschland gereist und habe Berlin, Hamburg und den Schwarzwald besucht.

Außerdem habe ich im Studentenklub Steffi kennen gelernt. Seit zwei Monaten sind wir ein Paar.

Ich möchte sehr gern für immer in Rostock bleiben – aber wie sage ich das meinen Eltern?

MARKS | DO NOT WRITE IN THIS MARGIN

Questions

(a) How long has Toby been studying in Germany?   1

(b) What did his parents think when he told them about his plans to study in Europe?   1

(c) Toby tells us that the atmosphere at Rostock University is very relaxed. What examples for this does Toby give in the text? Mention any **two** things.   2

(d) What advantage does Toby see in having a German university degree?   1

(e) According to the passage, how has Toby's time in Germany helped his personal development? Mention any **three** things.   3

(f) Who is Steffi?   1

(g) Think about why this article was published on the website. Tick the most appropriate reason for publication.   1

Toby wants to describe life as a student in Germany.	
Toby wants to describe the advantages and benefits of studying in Germany.	
Toby wants to describe the daily routine at a German university.	

Total marks 10

MARKS | DO NOT WRITE IN THIS MARGIN

Text 2

You then read an article on the same website about Germany as a tourist destination.

Deutschland — Reiseland

Die letzte Statistik des deutschen Tourismusverbandes ist der Beweis: Deutschland ist als Urlaubsland in Europa und in der Welt beliebt.

Die meisten Touristen kommen aus den Niederlanden, der Schweiz, den USA und Asien nach Deutschland. Sie besuchen sehr gern die Hauptstadt Berlin, weil sie die Geschichte der Stadt interessiert und sie die vielen Museen und Ausstellungen besuchen wollen. Außerdem ist Berlin im Vergleich zu anderen europäischen Hauptstädten sehr viel preiswerter bei bestem Service.

Ein neuer Trend ist der „Gesundheitstourismus". Besonders Gäste aus Brasilien, Russland, Indien und China kommen nach Deutschland, um sich hier medizinisch untersuchen und operieren zu lassen.

Leider interessieren sich nur 7% der Briten für Deutschland als Urlaubsland. Britische Touristen fahren lieber ans Mittelmeer — dabei gibt es auch in Deutschland saubere Strände, exzellente Wasserqualität in der Nord- und Ostsee, moderne Hotels mit erstklassigem Service und guten Preisen. Das Beste aber ist, dass man mit dem Flugzeug von Manchester, Edinburgh und London nur eine Stunde nach Deutschland fliegt — und im Sommer ist es oft genauso heiß wie in Spanien oder Südfrankreich.

Besuchen Sie Deutschland — es lohnt sich!

MARKS

Questions

(a) Are the following statements true or false? Tick the correct box.   2

	True	False
Germany is a popular holiday destination in Europe and in the world.		
Most of the tourists visiting Germany come from Australia.		

(b) What attracts tourists to Berlin? Mention any **two** things.   2

_____

_____

(c) According to the passage, what is the rather unusual reason why many tourists from Brazil, Russia, India and China visit Germany? Mention **one** thing.   1

_____

(d) Why is the number 7 mentioned in the text?   1

_____

(e) What does Germany have to offer British tourists? Mention any **three** things.   3

_____

_____

_____

(f) Think about why this article may have been published on the website. Tick the most appropriate reason for publication.   1

The article wants to show that Germany is a modern country.	
The article wants to promote Germany to British tourists as an alternative to holidays in the Mediterranean.	
The article wants to highlight a new type of tourism.	

Total marks 10

MARKS | DO NOT WRITE IN THIS MARGIN

Text 3

You then read an article about teenage mothers in Germany.

Mutter mit 17

Die Zahl der Teenager-Schwangerschaften in Deutschland steigt.

Anna ist jetzt 18 Jahre alt und hat einen einjährigen Sohn namens Marvin. Wie ist das Leben als junge Mutter?

„Es war schon ein totaler Schock, als der Schwangerschaftstest positiv war", sagt sie. Doch Anna hat sich für das Baby entschieden, obwohl die Eltern anfangs nicht dafür waren. Annas Mutter hatte Angst, dass ihre Tochter die Schule nicht beendet und dann auch nicht studieren kann. Aber Anna hat ehrgeizig und systematisch gearbeitet, damit sie trotz Marvins Geburt das Abitur machen konnte.

„Ohne meine Eltern hätte ich das nicht geschafft. Meine Mutter hat oft auf Marvin aufgepasst, wenn ich in der Schule war. Und mein Vater ist mit Marvin im Park spazieren gegangen, sodass ich Zeit und Ruhe für die Hausaufgaben hatte."

Und was ist mit Marvins Vater? „Wir haben uns kurz nach Marvins Geburt getrennt", sagt Anna, „aber ich bin seit drei Monaten mit Florian zusammen. Er akzeptiert Marvin ohne Probleme. Wir wollen bald in eine eigene Wohnung ziehen und ich hoffe, dass ich dann mein Kunststudium beginnen kann."

Annas Geschichte hat ein gutes Ende — leider ist das nicht oft so, wenn Teenager Eltern werden.

(a) What was Anna's reaction to the result of her pregnancy test?   1

_____

(b) Explain the worries that Anna's mother had. Mention **two** things.   2

_____

_____

(c) What did Anna do to pass her school leaving exams despite Marvin's birth? Mention **two** things.   2

_____

_____

Text 3 Questions (continued)

MARKS

(d) How did her parents support her? Mention **two** things.

2

_____

_____

(e) What are Anna's plans for the future? Mention **two** things.

2

_____

_____

(f) Overall, what impression on teenage pregnancy does the article give? Tick the most appropriate box.

1

The article promotes teenage pregnancies.	
The article is against teenage pregnancies.	
The article shows an example of family support for a teenage mother.	

Total marks 10

[END OF READING PAPER]

[BLANK PAGE]

National Qualifications
MODEL PAPER 3

German
Writing

Duration — 1 hour and 30 minutes

Total marks — 20

WRITING — 20 marks

Use **blue** or **black** ink.

You may use a German dictionary.

HODDER
GIBSON
LEARN MORE

WRITING — 20 marks

You are preparing an application for the job advertised below and you write an email **in German** to the company.

Mitarbeiter/Mitarbeiterin für Betriebsrestaurant gesucht

Der Franz-Wach-Personaldienst betreut mehr als Tausend Mitarbeiter von BMW München in der Mittagspause und bei vielen anderen Events.

Was sind Ihre Aufgaben?

Sie helfen bei der Essenausgabe und bereiten in der Küche Salate, Sandwiches und kleinere Speisen zu. Sie helfen beim Reinigen und Aufräumen der Küche sowie bei der Anlieferung und Lagerung der Lebensmittel.

Wie sollten Sie sein?

- freundlich, höflich, kontaktfreudig
- serviceorientiert und teamfähig
- gute Deutschkenntnisse
- Kenntnisse in anderen europäischen Sprachen

Berufserfahrung oder ein Arbeitspraktikum in einem Restaurant sind von Vorteil.

Was bieten wir Ihnen?

- ein professionelles Team
- eine freundliche Arbeitsatmosphäre
- €14 pro Stunde
- Schichtarbeit (auch abends)
- befristete oder unbefristete Arbeitsverträge
- sehr gute Karrierechancen
- Sozialversicherung

Wir freuen uns auf Ihre Bewerbung per E-mail an sabine.schmidt@franz-wach.com

---

To help you to write your e-mail, you have been given the following checklist of information to give about yourself and to ask about the job. You must include all of these points:

- Personal details (name, age, where you live)
- School/college/education experience until now
- Skills/interests you have which make you right for the job
- Related work experience
- How you can contribute towards kitchen work
- What you hope to get out of this experience

Use all of the above to help you write the e-mail **in German**, which should be approximately 120–150 words. You may use a **German** dictionary.

MARKS | DO NOT WRITE IN THIS MARGIN

ANSWER SPACE

ANSWER SPACE (continued)

MARKS

DO NOT
WRITE IN
THIS
MARGIN

ANSWER SPACE (continued)

ANSWER SPACE (continued)

[END OF WRITING PAPER]

ADDITIONAL SPACE FOR ANSWERS

ADDITIONAL SPACE FOR ANSWERS

National Qualifications
MODEL PAPER 3

German
Listening

Duration — 25 minutes

Total marks — 20

When you are told to do so, open your paper.

You will hear two items in German. **Before you hear each item, you will have one minute to study the question.** You will hear each item three times, with an interval of one minute between playings. You will then have time to answer the questions about it before hearing the next item.

Write your answers clearly, **in English**, in the spaces provided.

You may take notes as you are listening to the German.

Use **blue** or **black** ink.

You may NOT use a German dictionary.

HODDER
GIBSON
LEARN MORE

MARKS | DO NOT WRITE IN THIS MARGIN

Item 1

Your German friend Niklas tells you about his girlfriend, Helena.

(a) How old is Helena?   1

_____

(b) What did she wear when Niklas met her for the very first time? Mention **two** things.   2

_____

_____

(c) What happened after the school disco? Write any **one** thing.   1

_____

(d) Niklas tells us more about Helena's character. What does he like about her? Give **two** details.   2

_____

_____

(e) What are Helena and Niklas' next projects? Write any **one** thing.   1

_____

(f) What impression does Niklas give about his relationship to Helena? Tick the correct box.   1

Niklas cannot see himself staying with Helena.	
Niklas and Helena have a steady relationship.	
Niklas and Helena have no future plans.	

Total marks   8

MARKS | DO NOT WRITE IN THIS MARGIN

Item 2

You are listening to a podcast on the internet. Maria, a German teenager, is interviewed about her views on teenage relationships.

(a) How old is Maria?   **1**

_____

(b) Why does she not have a boyfriend? Mention any **two** things.   **2**

_____

_____

(c) Are the following statements true or false? Tick the correct box.   **3**

	True	False
Maria thinks that partners can share hobbies.		
Maria's sister has a boyfriend who likes football.		
Maria's sister is interested in football.		

(d) What does Maria say about the "perfect partner"? Mention any **three** things.   **3**

_____

_____

_____

(e) What is most important for Maria with regards to a relationship? Mention **three** things.   **3**

_____

_____

_____

Total marks 12

[END OF LISTENING PAPER]

[BLANK PAGE]

National Qualifications
MODEL PAPER 3

German
Listening Transcript

Duration — 25 minutes (approx)

This paper must not be seen by any candidates.

The material overleaf is provided for use in an emergency only (e.g. the recording or equipment proving faulty) or where permission has been given in advance by SQA for the material to be read to candidates with additional support needs. The material must be read exactly as printed.

Transcript – National 5

> **Instructions to reader(s):**
>
> For each item, read the English **once**, then read the German **three times**, with an interval of 1 minute between the three readings. On completion of the third reading pause for the length of time indicated in brackets after the item, to allow the candidates to write their answers.
>
> Where special arrangements have been agreed in advance to allow the reading of the material, those sections marked **(f)** should be read by a female speaker and those marked **(m)** by a male; those sections marked **(t)** should be read by the teacher.

(t) Item number one.

Your German friend, Niklas, tells you about his girlfriend, Helena.

You now have one minute to study the questions.

(m) Heute Abend kommt meine Freundin Helena. Sie ist 16 — so alt wie ich — und geht in meine Schule. Wir haben uns bei einer Schuldisko kennen gelernt. Sie hatte ein ganz tolles Outfit an - einen Minirock und ein schwarzes T-Shirt. Ich habe sie gefragt, ob sie mit mir tanzen möchte. Nach der Disko habe ich Helena nach Hause gebracht. Und am nächsten Wochenende sind wir dann ins Kino gegangen. Helena und ich verstehen uns sehr gut. Wir sind nicht immer einer Meinung — aber das ist doch normal.

Das Beste an Helena ist, dass sie nie launisch ist. Sie ist sehr geduldig und hilfsbereit. Helena ist auch sehr sportlich — so wie ich — und sie interessiert sich für Musik. Im nächsten Monat werden wir gemeinsam ein Konzert von Andreas Bourani besuchen. Das ist Helenas Lieblingssänger.

Unser größter Wunsch ist es, eine Rundreise durch Europa zu machen. Wir möchten sehr gern nach London fahren und auch den Eiffelturm in Paris besuchen. Wir haben beide einen Nebenjob und sparen das Geld für diese Reise. Ich bin sicher, dass das ein super tolles Erlebnis wird.

(2 minutes)

(t)   Item number two.

You are listening to a podcast on the internet. Maria, an Austrian teenager, is interviewed about her views on teenage relationships.

You now have one minute to study the questions.

(m/f) **Maria, du bist jetzt 17 Jahre alt. Hast du im Moment einen festen Freund?**

(f)   Naja, momentan bin ich single und ich finde das gut so.

(m/f) **Warum? Ist es nicht schöner, wenn man einen Partner hat?**

(f)   Ich bin der Meinung, dass ich im Moment keine Zeit für einen festen Partner habe. Es gibt einfach zu viele andere Dinge, die mir wichtiger sind: mein Schulabschluss, meine Hobbys und mein Freundeskreis.

(m/f) **Aber kann man Hobbys und Freunde nicht mit einem Partner teilen?**

(f)   Ich bin nicht sicher, ob das wirklich funktioniert. Meine Schwester hat seit zwei Jahren einen festen Freund. Er ist ein großer Fußballfan, sodass jedes Wochenende Fußball auf dem Programm steht — entweder im Stadion oder im Fernsehen. Meine Schwester geht gerne ins Theater oder ins Konzert — doch ihr Freund interessiert sich nicht dafür. Das würde mir nicht gefallen.

(m/f) **Wie sollte der perfekte Partner für dich sein?**

(f)   Also, einen perfekten Partner gibt es nicht. Niemand ist perfekt. Mein idealer Partner sollte mich zum Lachen bringen, wir sollten gleiche Interessen haben. Er sollte intelligent sein und Pläne für die Zukunft haben. Und er sollte nicht rauchen — denn Nichtraucherküsse schmecken besser.

(m/f) **Was ist für dich das Wichtigste in einer Partnerschaft?**

(f)   Das Wichtigste ist, dass man Vertrauen hat, dass man sich gegenseitig hilft und dass man kompromissbereit ist, wenn das notwendig ist.

(m/f) **Danke, Maria, für dieses Interview.**

(*2 minutes*)

(t)   **End of test.**
Now look over your answers.

[END OF TRANSCRIPT]

[BLANK PAGE]

N5

National Qualifications 2014

Mark

X734/75/01

German Reading

TUESDAY, 20 MAY

9:00 AM – 10:30 AM

Fill in these boxes and read what is printed below.

Full name of centre

Town

Forename(s)

Surname

Number of seat

Date of birth

Day	Month	Year

Scottish candidate number

Total marks — 30

Attempt ALL questions.

Write your answers clearly, in **English**, in the spaces provided in this booklet.

You may use a German dictionary.

Additional space for answers is provided at the end of this booklet. If you use this space you must clearly identify the question number you are attempting.

Use **blue** or **black** ink.

There is a separate question and answer booklet for Writing. You must complete your answer for Writing in the question and answer booklet for Writing.

Before leaving the examination room you must give both booklets to the Invigilator; if you do not, you may lose all the marks for this paper.

MARKS | DO NOT WRITE IN THIS MARGIN

Total marks — 30

Attempt ALL questions

Text 1

You read a magazine article about COOL-Centers, a recent development in German schools.

Im dritten Stock meiner Schule ist das COOL-Center. COOL heißt COoperatives Offenes Lernen, ein System, wo Schüler mit einem Lehrer in einer kleinen Gruppe arbeiten — es ist für die Schüler die Chance, ihre Arbeit mit anderen Schülern und Lehrern zu diskutieren und ihre Talente und Ideen zu entwickeln.

Das COOL-System hat viele Vorteile — in kleinen Gruppen kann man alles besser planen. Man hat viel Freiheit und man lernt, unabhängig zu sein.

Die siebzehnjährige Inge Schönefeld geht jeden Tag sehr gern ins COOL-Center: „Ich war schon immer ein bisschen schüchtern und in einer normalen Schulklasse habe ich nie etwas gesagt. Im COOL-Center dagegen habe ich alle Schüler in meiner Gruppe kennen gelernt und ich habe keine Angst, meine Meinung zu sagen."

„Auch für den späteren Beruf ist das COOL-Center etwas Positives: in der Gruppe lernt man, wie man sich am besten auf ein Interview vorbereitet. Ich habe zum Beispiel gelernt, dass das Aussehen immer sehr wichtig ist. Ich kann jetzt besser Augenkontakt halten, was für mich früher unmöglich war und vor allem habe ich gelernt, langsamer und deutlicher zu sprechen."

Questions

   (a) What does the COOL-Center give pupils the chance to do? Mention **two** things.

       2

_____

_____

   (b) What are the advantages of this system of learning? Mention any **two** things.

       2

_____

_____

MARKS | DO NOT WRITE IN THIS MARGIN

Text 1 Questions (continued)

(c) (i) What kind of person was Inge before she attended the COOL-Center? Mention **one** thing.

1

_____

(ii) In what way has Inge benefitted from being at the COOL-Center? Mention **two** things.

2

_____

_____

(d) The COOL-Center has helped Inge prepare for job interviews.

What has she learnt? Mention any **two** things.

2

_____

_____

(e) Reading the passage as a whole, who do you think the COOL-Center is intended for?

Tick (✓) the correct box.

1

Pupils with learning difficulties.	
Pupils who prefer to work independently.	
Pupils who like working with others.	

[Turn over

Text 2

MARKS

You read an article about the future of the cinema in Germany.

'Immer weniger Menschen gehen ins Kino' — *'Angst um die Zukunft der deutschen Filmindustrie'*.

Jens Pfarnauer ist Direktor eines kleinen Stadtkinos in Leipzig, und er weiß, dass es momentan ernste Probleme gibt: „Im vergangenen Jahr sind etwa 30% weniger Menschen durch die Tür gekommen. Woran liegt das? Die (inter)nationale Wirtschaftskrise spielt eine Rolle — viele Menschen haben einfach weniger Geld zur Verfügung."

Im großen Kinocenter am Stadtrand sieht es aber anders aus. „Bei uns läuft das Geschäft gut", so Karli Hägerich vom Odeonkino. „Wir haben genug Parkplätze für alle; an zwei Tagen in der Woche haben wir Karten im Sonderangebot und wir haben 10% Ermäßigung für regelmäßige Kinobesucher."

Es gibt natürlich viele Gründe, nicht mehr ins Kino zu gehen. Immer mehr Menschen haben große Bildschirme zu Hause. Man kann auf Pause drücken, wenn man will und man kann die neusten Kinohits direkt aus dem Internet herunterladen.

3D-Produktionen aber können eine bessere Zukunft für deutsche Kinos schaffen. Im letzten Jahr sind sieben deutsche 3D-Filme im Kino erschienen; das sind mehr als in jedem anderen Land – mit Ausnahme der USA!

Questions

(a) What statistic does Jens Pfarnauer quote to prove that the German film industry is in trouble? Complete the sentence.

1

Last year saw a 30% drop in _____.

(b) What reason is given for the film industry being in trouble? Mention any **one** thing.

1

_____

(c) Karli Hägerich has seen her cinema do well recently. What things have they done to attract business? Mention **three** things.

3

_____

_____

_____

MARKS

DO NOT WRITE IN THIS MARGIN

Text 2 Questions (continued)

(d) What reasons are there for staying in and watching movies at home? Mention **three** things.

3

_____

_____

_____

(e) Cinemas are hoping that 3D movies will help them survive. What shows that these films are doing well in Germany? Mention **two** things.

2

_____

_____

[Turn over

Text 3

MARKS

As part of a whole school project on Africa you have been asked to read this article in the German class.

Ohne Wasser gibt es kein Leben!

Das Wasser ist sehr wichtig für das Leben von Pflanzen, Tieren und Menschen. Wir brauchen es zum Kleiderwaschen, Kochen, Abspülen und Duschen.

In den meisten europäischen Ländern führt zu jedem Haus eine Leitung mit sauberem Wasser. Aber viele Menschen in Afrika haben kein Wasser in ihren Häusern. Sie holen sich das Wasser von einem Brunnen im Dorf oder sie müssen zum Fluss gehen. Oft ist das Wasser verschmutzt. Das ist sehr gefährlich, besonders für Kinder. Schmutziges Trinkwasser führt zu schweren Krankheiten und ist leider oft tödlich.

Aber auch in Deutschland gibt es Probleme mit verschmutztem Wasser. Viele deutsche Fabriken benutzen eine Menge chemische Produkte. Diese Produkte sind manchmal giftig und fließen in die Flüsse. Dann sterben Tausende von Fischen und Vögeln.

In Europa benutzen die Menschen zu viel Wasser. Ein Deutscher verbraucht täglich ungefähr 120 Liter Wasser, das sind zwölf Eimer voll mit Wasser. Wir sollten Wasser sparen, zum Beispiel: die Pflanzen im Garten nicht mehr als einmal die Woche giessen, den Wasserhahn nicht laufen lassen und die Spülmaschine nur anschalten, wenn sie voll ist.

Questions

(a) According to the article, what do people use water for?

Tick (✓) the **two** correct statements.   2

Washing the kitchen	
Washing clothes	
Showering	
Having a bath	

(b) In Africa lots of people have no water in their houses. Where do they fetch water from? Mention **two** things.   2

_____

_____

MARKS | DO NOT WRITE IN THIS MARGIN

Text 3 Questions (continued)

(c) Why is drinking dirty water dangerous for children? Mention **two** things.   2

_____

_____

(d) Why are German rivers polluted? Mention **two** things.   2

_____

_____

(e) Give any **two** examples of how we can save water.   2

_____

_____

[END OF QUESTION PAPER]

ADDITIONAL SPACE FOR ANSWERS

MARKS | DO NOT WRITE IN THIS MARGIN

ADDITIONAL SPACE FOR ANSWERS

[BLANK PAGE]

DO NOT WRITE ON THIS PAGE

N5

National Qualifications 2014

Mark

X734/75/02

German Writing

TUESDAY, 20 MAY

9:00 AM – 10:30 AM

Fill in these boxes and read what is printed below.

Full name of centre

Town

Forename(s)

Surname

Number of seat

Date of birth

Day   Month   Year

Scottish candidate number

Total marks — 20

Write your answer clearly, in **German**, in the space provided in this booklet.

You may use a German dictionary.

Additional space for answers is provided at the end of this booklet.

Use **blue** or **black** ink.

There is a separate question and answer booklet for Reading. You must complete your answers for Reading in the question and answer booklet for Reading.

Before leaving the examination room you must give both booklets to the Invigilator; if you do not, you may lose all the marks for this paper.

MARKS

DO NOT WRITE IN THIS MARGIN

Total marks — 20

You are preparing an application for the job advertised below and write an e-mail in **German** to the company.

Bürohilfe — Office Services

Otto-Brenner-Straße,
30159 Hannover-Mitte

Unsere Firma in Hannover sucht zuverlässige, motivierte

Mitarbeiter/-innen in unserem Büro

mit guten Deutsch- und Englischkenntnissen. Sie sollten auch gut organisieren können.

Sie können uns unter info@buerohilfe-officeservices.de für weitere Information kontaktieren, oder uns Ihre Bewerbung schicken.

To help you to write your e-mail, you have been given the following checklist.

You must include **all** of these points:

• Personal details (name, age, where you live)

• School/college/education experience until now

• Skills/interests you have which make you right for the job

• Related work experience

• Any links you may have with a German-speaking country

• Any questions you may have about the job

Use all of the above to help you write the e-mail in **German**. The e-mail should be approximately 120 – 150 words. You may use a German dictionary.

MARKS

ANSWER SPACE

[Turn over

ANSWER SPACE (continued)

ANSWER SPACE (continued)

[Turn over

MARKS | DO NOT WRITE IN THIS MARGIN

ANSWER SPACE (continued)

[END OF QUESTION PAPER]

MARKS | DO NOT WRITE IN THIS MARGIN

ADDITIONAL SPACE FOR ANSWERS

ADDITIONAL SPACE FOR ANSWERS

N5

National Qualifications 2014

Mark

X734/75/03

German Listening

TUESDAY, 20 MAY

10:50 AM – 11:15 AM (approx)

Fill in these boxes and read what is printed below.

Full name of centre

Town

Forename(s)

Surname

Number of seat

Date of birth

Day	Month	Year
D D	M M	Y Y

Scottish candidate number

Total marks — 20

Attempt ALL questions.

Write your answers clearly, in **English**, in the spaces provided in this booklet. Additional space for answers is provided at the end of this booklet. If you use this space you must clearly identify the question number you are attempting.

Use **blue** or **black** ink.

You will hear two items in German. **Before you hear each item, you will have one minute to study the questions.** You will hear each item three times, with an interval of one minute between playings. You will then have time to answer the questions before hearing the next item.

You may take notes as you are listening to the German, but only in this booklet.

You may NOT use a German dictionary.

You are not allowed to leave the examination room until the end of the test.

Before leaving the examination room you must give this booklet to the Invigilator; if you do not, you may lose all the marks for this paper.

MARKS | DO NOT WRITE IN THIS MARGIN

Total marks — 20

Attempt ALL questions

Item 1

Annika, a sixteen year old German girl, is talking about her part-time job.

(a) How long has she had her part-time job?   **1**

_____

(b) What does her job at the supermarket involve? Mention any **one** thing.   **1**

_____

(c) Annika talks about her working hours. Complete the sentence.   **1**

Annika works on Saturdays between 08.00 and _____.

(d) (i) How much does Annika earn per hour?   **1**

_____

(ii) What does she think of this?   **1**

_____

(e) What does Annika say about her workmates? Mention any **one** thing.   **1**

_____

(f) What does she think of the work she has to do? Mention any **one** thing.   **1**

_____

(g) Think about what Annika has said.

What do you think are the reasons behind her choosing to talk about her part-time job?

Tick (✓) the correct statement.   **1**

Annika wants to tell the listener . . .

. . . about how she works part-time and also manages to help out at home.	
. . . her opinion of the work she does and of what she gets paid.	
. . . that a job brings financial independence from her parents.	

Page two

MARKS | DO NOT WRITE IN THIS MARGIN

Item 2

Annika continues in an interview.

(a) What year is Annika in?   1

_____

(b) What time does Annika have to get up in the morning?   1

_____

(c) What do Annika and her friend, Bensu, do in the afternoon after school? Mention any **one** thing.   1

_____

(d) What surprises the interviewer?   1

_____

(e) Annika says French is her best subject. What reasons does she give for this?

Tick (✓) the **two** correct statements.   2

She gets good marks.	
She is motivated in French.	
She simply finds foreign languages easy.	
She works as well as she can.	

(f) History was her worst subject at school. Give **two** reasons why this was the case.   2

_____

_____

(g) Annika is unsure about her long-term plans.

What does she say about her best friend, Lara? Mention **two** things.   2

_____

_____

MARKS

Item 2 (continued)

(h) Annika is thinking about going to university.

What might she do after she graduates from university? Mention **two** things.

2

_____

_____

[END OF QUESTION PAPER]

ADDITIONAL SPACE FOR ANSWERS

MARKS | DO NOT WRITE IN THIS MARGIN

MARKS DO NOT WRITE IN THIS MARGIN

ADDITIONAL SPACE FOR ANSWERS

National Qualifications 2014

X734/75/13

German Listening Transcript

TUESDAY, 20 MAY

10:50 AM – 11:15 AM (approx)

This paper must not be seen by any candidate.

The material overleaf is provided for use in an emergency only (eg the recording or equipment proving faulty) or where permission has been given in advance by SQA for the material to be read to candidates with additional support needs. The material must be read exactly as printed.

Instructions to reader(s):

For each item, read the English once, then read the German **three times**, with an interval of 1 minute between the three readings. On completion of the third reading, pause for the length of time indicated in brackets after the item, to allow the candidates to write their answers.

Where special arrangements have been agreed in advance to allow the reading of the material, those sections marked **(f)** should be read by a female speaker and those marked **(m)** by a male; those sections marked **(t)** should be read by the teacher.

(t)   Item number one.

Annika, a sixteen year old German girl, is talking about her part-time job.

You now have one minute to study the questions for Item number one.

(f)   Mein Name ist Annika. Ich bin 16 und ich habe seit sechs Monaten einen Teilzeitjob. Ich arbeite in einem kleinen Supermarkt um die Ecke. Ich arbeite meistens an der Kasse, aber wir müssen auch jeden Abend die Regale auffüllen.

Ich arbeite donnerstags nach der Schule von sechs Uhr bis halb neun und samstags von acht Uhr bis halb fünf, also elf Stunden pro Woche. Ich verdiene €6,50 pro Stunde. Ich glaube, dass die Arbeit gut bezahlt ist.

Aber die Arbeit gefällt mir gar nicht: Die Mitarbeiter sind freundlich und hilfsbereit, aber es ist eine anstrengende Arbeit und so langweilig, weil ich so lange sitzen muss. Ich bekomme kein Taschengeld von meinen Eltern, aber ich verdiene ja ungefähr siebzig Euro die Woche.

Um etwas extra zu verdienen, muss ich bei der Hausarbeit helfen. Ich helfe meinem Vater beim Autowaschen und nach dem Abendessen muss ich die Spülmaschine einräumen und auch ausräumen. Ich finde das fair, weil meine Eltern ja beide arbeiten müssen.

(2 minutes)

(t) **Item number two.**

Annika continues in an interview.

You now have one minute to study the questions for Item number two.

(m) **Annika, in welche Klasse gehst du?**

(f) Ich bin im Moment in meinem letzten Jahr auf dem Immanuel-Kant-Gymnasium hier in Königsberg.

(m) **Gehst du gern in die Schule?**

(f) Oh ja, natürlich, aber ich muss sehr früh aufstehen, um Viertel vor sieben, weil die Schule um fünf vor acht anfängt. Daher nehme ich den Bus um Viertel nach sieben.

(m) **Und um wie viel Uhr ist die Schule aus?**

(f) Um halb eins, aber nachmittags haben wir AGs, das sind Arbeitsgemeinschaften: Bensu, eine Freundin aus meiner Klasse, und ich gehen zum Schulorchester, wo wir beide Geige spielen.

(m) **Wie viele Fächer hast du dieses Jahr?**

(f) Viele! Dieses Jahr habe ich Mathe, Englisch, Französisch, Italienisch und Deutsch, natürlich.

(m) **Was! Drei Fremdsprachen?**

(f) Ja, genau. Drei Fremdsprachen. Ich interessiere mich sehr für Fremdsprachen. Französisch ist mein bestes Fach: Ich glaube, dass ich motiviert bin, und ich arbeite, so gut ich kann. Und ich komme auch gut mit dem Lehrer aus: Er hat viel Geduld mit uns und hat einen guten Sinn für Humor.

(m) **Und dein schlechtestes Fach?**

(f) Das war letztes Jahr Geschichte. Kein Zweifel. Ich fand Geschichte schwierig und ich konnte mich im Unterricht nicht richtig konzentrieren.

(m) **Hast du Pläne für die Zukunft?**

(f) Ich weiß es noch nicht. Meine beste Freundin, Lara, war mit der Schule nicht zufrieden und hat dieses Jahr mit 16 die Schule verlassen. Sie hat einen Job bei einem Tierarzt gefunden und arbeitet jetzt mit Tieren.

(m) **Planst du, auf die Uni zu gehen?**

(f) Ja. Ich möchte vielleicht Englisch und Französisch an der Uni studieren.

(m) **Wo?**

(f) Keine Ahnung, aber nach Abschluss des Studiums hoffe ich, ein Gap-Year zu machen, vielleicht in Australien oder Neuseeland. Mein Traum wäre ein Job mit Kindern in einem Kindergarten oder in einer Grundschule . . .

(m) **Das ist eine schöne Idee, Annika. Danke.**

(f) Bitte sehr.

(2 minutes)

(t) **End of test.**

Now look over your answers.

[END OF TRANSCRIPT]

[BLANK PAGE]

NATIONAL 5

2015

N5

National Qualifications 2015

Mark

X734/75/01

German Reading

TUESDAY, 26 MAY

9:00 AM – 10:30 AM

Fill in these boxes and read what is printed below.

Full name of centre

Town

Forename(s)

Surname

Number of seat

Date of birth

Day   Month   Year   Scottish candidate number

Total marks — 30

Attempt ALL questions.

Write your answers clearly, in **English**, in the spaces provided in this booklet.

You may use a German dictionary.

Additional space for answers is provided at the end of this booklet. If you use this space you must clearly identify the question number you are attempting.

Use **blue** or **black** ink.

There is a separate question and answer booklet for Writing. You must complete your answer for Writing in the question and answer booklet for Writing.

Before leaving the examination room you must give both booklets to the Invigilator; if you do not, you may lose all the marks for this paper.

MARKS | DO NOT WRITE IN THIS MARGIN

Total marks — 30

Attempt ALL questions

Text 1

This passage is about exam stress and how to overcome this.

Prüfungsangst — dieses Gefühl, das jeder kennt. Viele Leute zittern, wenn sie das Wort „Prüfung" hören.

Wenn man sich auf eine Prüfung gut vorbereiten will, sollte man die Zeit gut planen. Man sollte zum Beispiel nicht stundenlang am Schreibtisch sitzen — eine kleine Pause alle neunzig Minuten ist die beste Belohnung.

Laura, 16, ist Schülerin am Schiller-Gymnasium in Hamburg: „Vor einer Prüfung habe ich meistens schwitzige Hände und habe keinen Appetit mehr. Wenn ich etwas lernen muss, schreibe ich eine Frage auf eine Karte und auf die Rückseite kommt dann die Antwort. Wenn ich eine mündliche Prüfung habe, übe ich mit einer Freundin. Das machen wir in einer neuen Umgebung, vielleicht in einem Café in der Stadt oder in der Schulbibliothek."

Lars Ritter ist Direktor der Rhein-Schule in Köln und er kennt die Sorgen, die Schüler in der Prüfungszeit erleben: „Wir sagen den Schülern, dass Prüfungsangst normal und sogar nötig ist. Ohne Angst würde man die Prüfungssituation nicht ernst nehmen. Negative Gedanken so wie: ,Durchfallen wäre eine Katastrophe', muss man vergessen. Viel besser ist es, wenn man denkt: ,Ich habe mich auf die Prüfung vorbereitet und ich hoffe, dass ich eine gute Note bekomme.'"

Questions

(a) How do many people react to the mention of exams? Complete the following sentence.

1

Lots of people _____ when they hear the word "exam".

(b) What is the best way to plan your time for studying? Give **two** details.

2

_____

_____

MARKS | DO NOT WRITE IN THIS MARGIN

Text 1 Questions (continued)

(c) How does Laura react before exams? State any **one** thing.   1

_____

(d) (i) How does she prepare for **speaking** exams?   1

_____

   (ii) Where does she do this? State any **one** thing.   1

_____

(e) What does headmaster Lars Ritter say to his pupils about exam nerves?
    State **two** things.   2

_____

_____

(f) Lars Ritter gives examples of the negative and positive thoughts students
    can have about exams.

   (i) Which negative thought does he mention?   1

_____

   (ii) Give **one** of the positive thoughts students might have.   1

_____

[Turn over

MARKS | DO NOT WRITE IN THIS MARGIN

Text 2

Lisa Wiedermann recently visited India and spent time at an international school.

Im Februar dieses Jahres hatte ich die Gelegenheit, mit einer Gruppe nach Indien zu fahren. Die Organisation „Asien-Kontakt" hat die Hälfte meiner Reisekosten bezahlt. Diese Organisation will Kontakt zwischen Jugendlichen in Indien und Deutschland fördern — sowie auch Toleranz zwischen den beiden Ländern.

An meinem ersten Tag in der indischen Schule habe ich eine schöne Blumenkette bekommen — das ist ein Zeichen der Freundschaft. Wir hatten natürlich auch Geschenke und Infomaterial aus Deutschland mitgebracht.

Ich war sehr beeindruckt von der Gastfreundlichkeit unserer indischen Gastgeber. Sie haben so viele Ausflüge für uns organisiert, um uns das Land und Leute näher zu bringen, jeden Abend gab es ein richtiges Fest mit indischen Spezialitäten und wir haben sogar das indische Parlamentsgebäude in Neu Delhi besucht.

Für mich war es erstaunlich, dass sich so viele Leute in Indien für Deutschland und die Deutschen interessieren. In der Schule zeigten uns zwei Schülerinnen die Bücher, die sie ganz auf Deutsch gelesen hatten. Drei Jungen erzählten uns über die zwei Wochen, die sie bei einer Kirchengruppe in Hamburg verbracht hatten.

Nächstes Jahr möchte ich mit meiner Familie zurückfahren, um dieses schöne Land besser kennen zu lernen.

Questions

(a) In what way did the organisation *Asien-Kontakt* help Lisa Wiedermann?   1

_____

_____

MARKS | DO NOT WRITE IN THIS MARGIN

Text 2 Questions (continued)

(b) What does this organisation want to promote? State **two** things.

2

_____

_____

(c) Why was Lisa given a necklace of flowers on her first day at the Indian school?

1

_____

_____

(d) Lisa was impressed by Indian hospitality.

What did the Indian hosts arrange for the German visitors? State **three** things.

3

_____

_____

_____

(e) What showed Lisa that Indian people have an interest in Germany?

Complete the sentences.

2

Two pupils showed her books which _____

_____.

Three boys told her about _____

_____.

(f) Reading the passage as a whole, why do you think Lisa has chosen to write it?

Tick (✓) the correct box.

1

She wants to move to India when she is older.	
She wants to promote understanding between the two countries.	
She wants to promote India as a holiday destination.	

MARKS | DO NOT WRITE IN THIS MARGIN

Text 3

Sara, a German girl, is writing about her work placement and how to plan for the future.

Meine Lehrer in der Schule haben mir bei meiner Berufswahl sehr geholfen. Sie haben mit mir und meinen Eltern gesprochen, denn sie wissen, dass meine Noten in der Schule nicht immer gut sind. Sie sagen aber, dass ich eine gute Schülerin bin und das finde ich toll. Ich habe ein Arbeitspraktikum in einer Bäckerei gemacht und das hat großen Spaß gemacht. Die Arbeit ist sehr kreativ, man kann mit den Händen arbeiten, was ich sehr gut finde, und man kann auch mit neuen Ideen experimentieren. Als ich mein Praktikum machte, hatte ich eine gute Idee für einen Weihnachtskuchen und mein Chef hat gesagt: „Ja, warum nicht?" Mein Kuchen hat sehr gut geschmeckt und sie haben ihn in der Konditorei verkauft. Ich war so stolz.

Schon in der Schulzeit sollte man an eine künftige Karriere denken. Das ist nicht immer so einfach, denn man hat oft andere, wichtigere Dinge zu tun, wie zum Beispiel Prüfungen ablegen oder neue Talente entdecken und entwickeln. Viele Schüler fühlen sich einfach zu jung und unerfahren, um an ihre Berufswahl zu denken.

Ein Arbeitspraktikum ist aber eine gute Möglichkeit, Einblicke in die Arbeitswelt zu bekommen. Man kann durch eigene Erfahrung lernen und persönliche Kontakte schließen.

Questions

(a) Which of the following statements best describes Sara's work in school?

Tick (✓) the **one** correct statement.   1

Sara works well in school and is a high achiever.	
Sara's work is not perfect but she is a good pupil.	

(b) Why did Sara enjoy her work placement in the bakery? Give **three** reasons.   3

_____

_____

_____

MARKS | DO NOT WRITE IN THIS MARGIN

Text 3 Questions (continued)

(c) Why was Sarah proud of her Christmas cake? State **two** things.　　2

_____

_____

(d) What is often more important to school pupils than thinking about a future career? State **two** things.　　2

_____

_____

(e) There are many advantages of doing a work placement. State any **two** of these.　　2

_____

_____

[END OF QUESTION PAPER]

MARKS | DO NOT WRITE IN THIS MARGIN

ADDITIONAL SPACE FOR ANSWERS

MARKS | DO NOT WRITE IN THIS MARGIN

ADDITIONAL SPACE FOR ANSWERS

[BLANK PAGE]

DO NOT WRITE ON THIS PAGE

[BLANK PAGE]

DO NOT WRITE ON THIS PAGE

[BLANK PAGE]

DO NOT WRITE ON THIS PAGE

National Qualifications 2015

Mark

X734/75/02

German Writing

TUESDAY, 26 MAY

9:00 AM – 10:30 AM

Fill in these boxes and read what is printed below.

Full name of centre

Town

Forename(s)

Surname

Number of seat

Date of birth

Day   Month   Year   Scottish candidate number

Total marks — 20

Write your answer clearly, in **German**, in the space provided in this booklet.

You may use a German dictionary.

Additional space for answers is provided at the end of this booklet.

Use **blue** or **black** ink.

There is a separate question and answer booklet for Reading. You must complete your answers for Reading in the question and answer booklet for Reading.

Before leaving the examination room you must give both booklets to the Invigilator; if you do not, you may lose all the marks for this paper.

Total marks — 20

You are preparing an application for the job advertised below and you write an e-mail in **German** to the company.

Hotel „Sonnenhof"

Annagasse 15 — 90402 Nürnberg

Die Leitung des Hotels „Sonnenhof" sucht sofort freundliche, motivierte, junge Leute als

Mitarbeiter/-innen an der **Hotelrezeption**

Sie sollten gute Sprachkenntnisse in Englisch und Deutsch haben und sollten gut mit unseren Gästen umgehen können.

Sie können uns unter info@hotel-sonnenhof.de für weitere Information kontaktieren und uns Ihre Bewerbung schicken.

Ihre Bewerbung sollte folgende Information enthalten:

To help you to write your e-mail, you have been given the following checklist.

You must include **all** of these points:

- Personal details (name, age, where you live)
- School/college/education experience until now
- Skills/interests you have which make you right for the job
- Related work experience
- Any links you may have with a German-speaking country
- Your future education/career plans

Use all of the above to help you write the e-mail in **German**. The e-mail should be approximately 120–150 words. You may use a German dictionary.

MARKS | DO NOT WRITE IN THIS MARGIN

ANSWER SPACE

ANSWER SPACE (continued)

MARKS | DO NOT WRITE IN THIS MARGIN

ANSWER SPACE (continued)

MARKS | DO NOT WRITE IN THIS MARGIN

ANSWER SPACE (continued)

[END OF QUESTION PAPER]

ADDITIONAL SPACE FOR ANSWERS

MARKS | DO NOT WRITE IN THIS MARGIN

ADDITIONAL SPACE FOR ANSWERS

N5

National Qualifications 2015

X734/75/03

German Listening

TUESDAY, 26 MAY

10:50 AM – 11:15 AM (approx)

Fill in these boxes and read what is printed below.

Full name of centre

Town

Forename(s)

Surname

Number of seat

Date of birth

Day	Month	Year	Scottish candidate number

Total marks — 20

Attempt ALL questions.

You will hear two items in German. **Before you hear each item, you will have one minute to study the questions.** You will hear each item three times, with an interval of one minute between playings. You will then have time to answer the questions before hearing the next item.

You may NOT use a German dictionary.

Write your answers clearly, in **English**, in the spaces provided in this booklet. Additional space for answers is provided at the end of this booklet. If you use this space you must clearly identify the question number you are attempting.

Use **blue** or **black** ink.

You are not allowed to leave the examination room until the end of the test.

Before leaving the examination room you must give this booklet to the Invigilator; if you do not, you may lose all the marks for this paper.

MARKS | DO NOT WRITE IN THIS MARGIN

Total marks — 20

Attempt ALL questions

Item 1

Erik is talking about life at home and why he has two bedrooms.

(a) When is Erik's birthday? Tick (✓) the correct box.   **1**

3rd August	
13th August	
31st August	

(b) When did Erik's parents separate?   **1**

_____

_____

(c) When does Erik live with his father? State any **two** things.   **2**

_____

_____

(d) What are the arrangements for Erik at Christmas? State **two** things.   **2**

_____

_____

(e) Why is Maths Erik's favourite subject?   **1**

_____

_____

(f) Overall, how does Erik feel about life at the moment?

Tick (✓) the most appropriate statement.   **1**

He is unhappy.	
He has his ups and downs.	
He is positive.	

Item 2

Erik continues in an interview.

(a) Who is Martin?

    1

_____

(b) What does he say about his relationship with Martin?

State any **one** thing.

    1

_____

_____

(c) What do Erik's parents do for a living? Complete the grid.

    2

Mother	
Father	

(d) Why can't Erik and Martin have a dog?

    1

_____

_____

(e) (i) **Apart from** electric guitar, what instrument does Erik play?

    1

_____

(ii) How long has he been playing this instrument?

    1

_____

(f) What does Erik say about his friends at school? State any **three** things.

    3

_____

_____

_____

(g) What do Erik and his friend do in their spare time? State any **two** things.

    2

_____

_____

[END OF QUESTION PAPER]

MARKS DO NOT WRITE IN THIS MARGIN

ADDITIONAL SPACE FOR ANSWERS

MARKS | DO NOT WRITE IN THIS MARGIN

ADDITIONAL SPACE FOR ANSWERS

[BLANK PAGE]

DO NOT WRITE ON THIS PAGE

[BLANK PAGE]

DO NOT WRITE ON THIS PAGE

[BLANK PAGE]

DO NOT WRITE ON THIS PAGE

National
Qualifications
2015

X734/75/13

**German
Listening Transcript**

TUESDAY, 26 MAY

10:50 AM – 11:15 AM

This paper must not be seen by any candidate.

The material overleaf is provided for use in an emergency only (eg the recording or equipment proving faulty) or where permission has been given in advance by SQA for the material to be read to candidates with additional support needs. The material must be read exactly as printed.

> **Instructions to reader(s):**
>
> For each item, read the English once, then read the German **three times**, with an interval of 1 minute between the three readings. On completion of the third reading, pause for the length of time indicated in brackets after the item, to allow the candidates to write their answers.
>
> Where special arrangements have been agreed in advance to allow the reading of the material, those sections marked **(f)** should be read by a female speaker and those marked **(m)** by a male; those sections marked **(t)** should be read by the teacher.

(t)   Item number one.

Erik is talking about life at home and why he has two bedrooms.

You now have one minute to study the questions for Item number one.

(m) Mein Name ist Erik und ich bin 15. Ich habe am 13. August Geburtstag. Ich wohne in einem Haus in Nürnberg-Galgenhof — das ist ein Vorort von Nürnberg. Ich habe zwei Schlafzimmer, das eine bei meiner Mutter hier in Nürnberg und das zweite bei meinem Vater in Fürth. Fürth liegt nur acht Kilometer von Nürnberg entfernt.

Meine Eltern haben sich vor vier Jahren getrennt, als ich elf Jahre alt war. Ich lebe die meiste Zeit bei meiner Mutter. Aber mittwochs, jedes zweite Wochenende und vier Wochen in den Schulferien wohne ich bei meinem Vater und seiner Freundin.

Ich verbringe Weihnachten immer bei meiner Mutter. Meinen Vater besuche ich immer zwei Tage später. So bekomme ich zweimal Geschenke. Das ist toll!

Ich gehe in die zehnte Klasse eines Gymnasiums in Nürnberg. Am besten gefallen mir die Fächer Kunst, Musik und Mathe. Mathe ist mein Lieblingsfach und ich bekomme immer gute Noten. Und natürlich auch Sport! Außerdem spiele ich Fußball und Volleyball im Verein.

(2 minutes)

MARKS

(t) Item number two.

Erik continues in an interview.

You now have one minute to study the questions for Item number two.

(f) Erik, hast du Geschwister?

(m) Ja, zu Hause sind wir zu dritt. Meine Mutter, mein kleiner Bruder Martin und ich. Martin ist zwei Jahre jünger als ich.

(f) Kommst du mit Martin gut aus?

(m) Ja, klar! Wir kommen miteinander ganz gut aus — er kann mir ab und zu auf die Nerven gehen, zum Beispiel, wenn er in mein Zimmer kommt, ohne an die Tür zu klopfen, aber ich mag ihn.

(f) Was machen deine Eltern beruflich?

(m) Meine Mutter ist Sekretärin in einem Büro in der Stadtmitte und mein Vater ist Polizist. Meine Mutter ist klein und schlank. Sie hat blonde Haare und grüne Augen. Mein Vater ist 42 und meine Mutter ist zwei Jahre jünger.

(f) Habt ihr Haustiere?

(m) Ja, wir haben zwei Goldfische. Martin und ich möchten sehr gerne einen Hund, aber meine Mutter ist gegen Hunde allergisch!

(f) Du interessierst dich für Musik. Spielst du ein Instrument?

(m) Ja, ich spiele seit drei Jahren Klavier und seit einem Jahr elektrische Gitarre. Ich gehe mit zwei Freunden zur Musikgruppe in der Stadtmitte, wo wir zusammen Musik machen.

(f) Hast du viele Freunde in der Schule?

(m) Ja, ich habe drei oder vier echt gute Freunde. Sie sind oft ziemlich laut, aber ich finde sie auch sehr lustig und wir haben die gleichen Interessen.

(f) Treibt ihr auch viel Sport?

(m) Ja, wir gehen zusammen im Stadtpark joggen, machen in der Gegend Radtouren und spielen in der Fußballmannschaft der Schule — ich bin Stürmer. Wir gehen auch regelmäßig ins Kino.

(f) Was für Filme seht ihr gerne?

(m) Wir sehen uns gern Abenteuerfilme an. Mein Lieblingsschauspieler ist Will Smith und mein Lieblingsfilm ist «X-Men».

(f) Danke, Erik!

(m) Kein Problem!

(2 minutes)

(t) End of test.

Now look over your answers.

[END OF TRANSCRIPT]

[BLANK PAGE]

SQA AND HODDER GIBSON NATIONAL 5 GERMAN 2015

Reading

Text 1

1. (a) (For) two months   1

  (b) • great/cool people
      • great/cool service
      • (really) good food   3

  (c) • She loves Hamburg/She is totally enthusiastic about
        the city/town/place/She is doing work experience
        there
      • Hamburg has more than two million inhabitants
      • There are many parks
      • There is a lot of water in Hamburg
      • You don't think you live in a city
      (any three out of five)   3

  (d) Positive/good relationship because
      • They are friendly
      • They are helpful
      • They go out/to the cinema/to one of the clubs in
        the Reeperbahn at the weekend
      (correct evaluation any one out of three)   2

  (e)

The text gives an overall positive view of Gemma's work experience in Hamburg.	✗
The text gives an overall negative view of Gemma's work experience in Hamburg.	

                                                                                                1

Text 2

2. (a) • The number of bi-national couples is rising in
        Germany
      • Every fourth child born in Germany has one non-
        German parent
      (any one out of two)   1

  (b) • five years ago
      • at an environmental conference/in Hanover   2

  (c) • to get to know Brian's family better
      • to get to know Brian's home country better   2

  (d) • improve his German
      • look for/apply for a job   2

  (e) • He has a university degree/an academic degree/a
        university qualification
      • He speaks English and German   2

  (f)

Brian is missing Scotland a lot and wants to move back to Glasgow.	
Brian is happy in Berlin and finds it easy to visit Glasgow if he wants to.	✗

                                                                                                1

Text 3

3. (a) • He is an only child./He has no siblings
      • Life can be boring when you are an only child
      (any one out of two)   1

  (b) • Having a dog means responsibility/A dog owner has
        responsibility   1

  (c) • You must walk the dog three times a day
      • You must take him to the vet's
      • You must train him properly (so that there are no
        problems with the neighbours/to avoid problems
        with the neighbours)   3

  (d) • He bought a book about how to raise a dog/dog
        training
      • He found a dog school nearby via the internet/He
        takes Bonzo to a dog school once a week   2

  (e) • Bonzo keeps Thomas fit/He can run with him
        through the woods or the park/He can jog with him
        without problems   1

  (f) • Thomas recommends a dog as a pet
      • A dog is better than a/any fitness studio/A dog
        owner has super fun/lots of fun with the dog   2

Writing

General Marking Principles

Candidates will write a piece of extended writing in the modern language by addressing six bullet points. These bullet points will follow on from a job-related scenario. The bullet points will cover the four contexts of society, learning, employability and culture to allow candidates to use and adapt learned material. The first four bullet points will be the same each year and the last two will change to suit the scenario. Candidates need to address these "unpredictable bullet points" in detail to access the full range of marks.

Category	Mark	Content	Accuracy	Language resource – variety, range, structures
Very good	20	The job advert has been addressed in a full and balanced way. The candidate uses detailed language. The candidate addresses the advert completely and competently, **including information in response to both unpredictable bullet points.** A range of verbs/ verb forms, tenses and constructions is used. Overall this comes over as a competent, well thought-out and serious application for the job.	The candidate handles all aspects of grammar and spelling accurately, although the language may contain one or two minor errors. Where the candidate attempts to use language more appropriate to Higher, a slightly higher number of inaccuracies need not detract from the overall very good impression.	The candidate is comfortable with the first person of the verb and generally uses a different verb in each sentence. Some modal verbs and infinitives may be used. There is good use of adjectives, adverbs and prepositional phrases and, where appropriate, word order. There may be a range of tenses. The candidate uses co-ordinating conjunctions and/or subordinate clauses where appropriate. The language of the e-mail flows well.
Good	16	The job advert has been addressed competently. There is less evidence of detailed language. The candidate uses a reasonable range of verbs/verb forms. Overall, the candidate has produced a genuine, reasonably accurate attempt at applying for the specific job, **even though he/she may not address one of the unpredictable bullet points.**	The candidate handles a range of verbs fairly accurately. There are some errors in spelling, adjective endings and, where relevant, case endings. Use of accents is less secure, where appropriate. Where the candidate is attempting to use more complex vocabulary and structures, these may be less successful, although basic structures are used accurately. There may be one or two examples of inaccurate dictionary use, especially in the unpredictable bullet points.	There may be repetition of verbs. There may be examples of listing, in particular when referring to school/ college experience, without further amplification. There may be one or two examples of a co-ordinating conjunction, but most sentences are simple sentences. The candidate keeps to more basic vocabulary, particularly in response to either or both unpredictable bullet points.

Category	Mark	Content	Accuracy	Language resource — variety, range, structures
Satisfactory	12	The job advert has been addressed fairly competently. The candidate makes limited use of detailed language. The language is fairly repetitive and uses a limited range of verbs and fixed phrases, e.g. *I like, I go, I play*. The candidate copes fairly well with areas of personal details, education, skills, interests and work experience but does not deal fully with the two unpredictable bullet points **and indeed may not address either or both of the unpredictable bullet points.** On balance however the candidate has produced a satisfactory job application in the specific language.	The verbs are generally correct, but may be repetitive. There are quite a few errors in other parts of speech — gender of nouns, cases, singular/plural confusion, for instance. Prepositions may be missing, e.g. *I go the town.* Overall, there is more correct than incorrect.	The candidate copes with the first and third person of a few verbs, where appropriate. A limited range of verbs is used. Sentences are basic and mainly brief. There is minimal use of adjectives, probably mainly after *is* e.g. *Chemistry is interesting.* The candidate has a weak knowledge of plurals. There may be several spelling errors, e.g. reversal of vowel combinations.
Unsatisfactory	8	The job advert has been addressed in an uneven manner and/or with insufficient use of detailed language. The language is repetitive, e.g. *I like, I go, I play* may feature several times. There may be little difference between Satisfactory and Unsatisfactory. **Either or both of the unpredictable bullet points may not have been addressed.** There may be one sentence which is not intelligible to a sympathetic native speaker.	Ability to form tenses is inconsistent. There are errors in many other parts of speech — gender of nouns, cases, singular/plural confusion, for instance. Several errors are serious, perhaps showing mother tongue interference. The detail in the unpredictable bullet points may be very weak. Overall, there is more incorrect than correct.	The candidate copes mainly only with the personal language required in bullet points 1 and 2. The verbs *is* and *study* may also be used correctly. Sentences are basic. An English word may appear in the writing. There may be an example of serious dictionary misuse.

Category	Mark	Content	Accuracy	Language resource — variety, range, structures
Poor	4	The candidate has had considerable difficulty in addressing the job advert. There is little evidence of the use of detailed language. Three or four sentences may not be understood by a sympathetic native speaker. **Either or both of the unpredictable bullet points may not have been addressed.**	Many of the verbs are incorrect. There are many errors in other parts of speech — personal pronouns, gender of nouns, cases, singular/plural confusion, prepositions, for instance. The language is probably inaccurate throughout the writing.	The candidate cannot cope with more than one or two basic verbs. The candidate displays almost no knowledge of the present tense of verbs. Verbs used more than once may be written differently on each occasion. Sentences are very short. The candidate has a very limited vocabulary. Several English words may appear in the writing. There are examples of serious dictionary misuse.
Very poor	0	The candidate is unable to address the job advert. **The two unpredictable bullet points may not have been addressed.** Very little is intelligible to a sympathetic native speaker.	Virtually nothing is correct.	The candidate may only cope with the verbs *to have* and *to be*. Very few words are written correctly in the modern language. English words are used. There may be several examples of mother tongue interference. There may be several examples of serious dictionary misuse.

NATIONAL 5 GERMAN MODEL PAPER 1

Listening

Item 1

1. (a) Anna is sixteen years old   1

(b) • She is an exchange student./She is on an exchange   1

(c) • It is a big town/city
   • It is in the west of Germany/in West Germany
   • Bremen is famous for football
   • Bremen is famous for the Bremen town musicians
   • She likes living in Bremen
   (any two out of five)   2

(d) Anna goes to ballet class (once a week)   1

(e) • friendly
   • funny/jolly
   • a bit moody
   • not always on time
   (any two for one mark)   1

(f) They are Anna's dogs   1

(g)

Anna is homesick and is not enjoying her stay in St Andrews.	
Anna is enjoying her stay in St Andrews and would like to return as a student.	✗
Anna cannot see herself coming back to Scotland again.	

   1

Item 2

2. (a) • Edinburgh is a cool/fantastic city
   • Edinburgh has an interesting history
   • Edinburgh has many sights
   (any two out of three)   2

(b)

Paul's host family lives on the outskirts in the west of Edinburgh.	✗
Paul shared a room in the house.	
Paul had a TV and a computer in the room.	✗
Paul had no contact to his German family and friends.	

   2

(c) • In Scotland there are comprehensive schools
   • School in Scotland starts at nine o'clock
   • School in Scotland finishes at half past three
   • The school day in Scotland is long
   • You have lunch in Scottish schools
   (any three out of five)   3

(d) He went to rugby training   1

(e) • They walked along the beach/on the beach
   • They played golf   2

(f) • You learn about/get to know a new lifestyle
   • You learn about/get to know a new culture
   • You become more confident
   • You become more independent
   • Paul's English has improved
   • He has learned to play rugby and golf
   (any two out of six)   2

NATIONAL 5 GERMAN MODEL PAPER 2

Reading

Text 1

1. (a) • Kissing is relaxing/kissing relaxes
   • Kissing makes you happy   1

(b) • One burns 12 calories in an intensive kiss
   • More than 30 muscles in the face and neck are active when kissing
   • Kissing prevents wrinkles
   • Kissing protects teeth from decay
   • Kissing decreases/lowers stress hormones
   • Kissing strengthens the immune system
   (any three out of six)   3

(c) It is (a bit) like sport   1

(d) The person is somebody special (for him)   1

(e) • On the 6th July
   • On the International Day of Kisses
   (any one out of two)   1

(f) • She read a lot (about kissing)
   • She heard a lot (about kissing)
   • She researched on the internet (about kissing)
   (any two out of three)   2

(g)

The author of the article wants to entertain the readers.	
The author of the article wants to highlight that kissing has positive effects on people's health.	✗
The author wants to encourage young people to talk about health issues.	

   1

Text 2

2. (a) YOU – this is the most important exhibition with focus on youth culture in Germany   2

(b) More than 100 000 young people visit YOU every year/every summer   1

(c) • They can see national and international music stars
   • They can have a party with a DJ/with DJs
   • They can present their own talent (on stage)/take part in a talent competition
   • They can try many kinds of sports
   (any two out of four)   2

(d) • Education
   • Career
   • Future
   (any two out of three)   2

(e) • Young people should organise their lives actively/take part/take things on/try things out
   • Young people should show initiative
   (any one out of two)   1

(f) Purchase/buy/get tickets (online)   1

(g)

The article wants to encourage young people to visit this exhibition.	✗
The article shows young people what they can do in the future.	
The article promotes Berlin as a city for young people.	

1

Text 3

3. (a) • He likes to get up early
   • He has no problems delivering good work/working well/ doing a good job/to performing well
   • He (really) likes driving (cars)
   (any two out of three) 2

   (b) • He enjoys making people happy
   • He enjoys delivering parcels (with presents from family and friends) at Christmas
   (any one out of two) 1

   (c) • At school she did work experience at a vet's
   • She did not enjoy the work there/her work experience 2

   (d) • Martina has many patients.
   • She often does not have (enough) time 2

   (e) • One must ask if the job is interesting
   • One must ask if there are enough jobs
   • The labour market is important
   • Not to be unemployed is important/She does not want to be unemployed
   (any two out of four) 2

   (f)

Bernd	✗
Martina	
Britta	

   1

Writing

Please see the assessment criteria for Writing on pages 154–6.

Listening

Item 1

1. (a) Students 1

   (b) • Netbooks are practical
   • One is flexible/mobile with a netbook 2

   (c) Since she was ten/since her tenth birthday 1

   (d) • Make phone calls
   • Send texts
   • Surf the internet
   • Check e-mails
   • Take pictures/photos
   • Make videos/record videos
   • Connect to/go to Facebook and Twitter
   (any three out of seven) 3

   (e)

Simone thinks that modern technology is not really important.	
Simone's mobile phone is important to her and she loves to meet her friends online.	
Simone's mobile phone is important to her, but she prefers to meet her friends face-to-face rather than online.	✗

   1

Item 2

2. (a) Two hours 1

   (b) • Christian checked his e-mails
   • He was on Facebook
   • He downloaded music
   • He watched some videos on Youtube/online
   (any three out of four) 3

   (c) • The programmes on TV are a disaster/a catastrophe
   • There are only boring talent shows on
   • There are only soap operas on
   • The TV schedule/programming is not for him at the moment
   (any two out of four) 2

   (d)

Christian likes the cinema a lot.	
Christian prefers to watch DVDs at home.	✗
Christian thinks that sitting at home is not boring.	✗
Christian does not have many friends at school.	

   2

   (e) • He can contact his friends on his mobile phone
   • They send each other text messages
   • They chat to each other on Facebook
   (any two out of three) 2

   (f) • He can listen to music on his mobile phone
   • He can test/try his new/latest Nintendo DS game 2

NATIONAL 5 GERMAN
MODEL PAPER 3

Reading

Text 1

1. (a) For two years — 1

(b) They were not enthusiastic/They did not like the idea/plan — 1

(c) • You can choose your courses yourself
• You can put together your own timetable
• If there are any problems, you can go to your tutor
• If there are any problems you can go to the student council
(any two out of four) — 2

(d) Very good career opportunities/chances — 1

(e) • He speaks German fluently/without problems
• He has become more independent
• He has become more open-minded/outward-looking
• He has travelled around Germany/seen different places in Germany
(any three out of four) — 3

(f) Toby's girlfriend/his girlfriend — 1

(g)

Toby wants to describe life as a student in Germany.	
Toby wants to describe the advantages and benefits of studying in Germany.	✗
Toby wants to describe the daily routine at a German university.	

1

Text 2

2. (a)

	True	False
Germany is a popular holiday destination in Europe and in the world.	✗	
Most of the tourists visiting Germany come from Australia.		✗

2

(b) • They are interested in the history of the city
• They want to visit the (many) museums and exhibitions
• Berlin is cheaper than other European capitals (with the best service)
(any two out of three) — 2

(c) • They undergo medical examination
• They come for (medical) operations
• They are health tourists
(any one out of three) — 1

(d) Only seven per cent of British people are interested in a holiday in Germany/in Germany as a holiday country/destination — 1

(e) • Clean beaches
• Excellent water quality in North Sea and Baltic Sea
• Modern hotels
• First-class service
• Good prices

• only an hour away by plane
• summers can be as hot as in Spain or the south of France
(any three out of seven) — 3

(f)

The article wants to show that Germany is a modern country.	
The article wants to promote Germany to British tourists as an alternative to holidays on the Mediterranean Sea.	✗
The article wants to highlight a new way of tourism.	

1

Text 3

3. (a) She was totally shocked/total shock — 1

(b) • Her mother was worried that Anna would not finish school
• She was worried that Anna would be unable to study — 2

(c) • She was ambitious
• She worked systematically — 2

(d) • Her mother looked after Marvin when Anna was in school
• Her father took Marvin for a walk in the park/to the park so that Anna had (peace and) time for homework/was able to do her homework — 2

(e) • She wants a flat of her own (with her boyfriend Florian and Marvin)
• She wants to study Art — 2

(f)

The article promotes teenage pregnancies.	
The article is against teenage pregnancies.	
The article shows an example of family support for a teenage mother.	✗

1

Writing

Please see the assessment criteria for Writing on pages 154–6.

NATIONAL 5 GERMAN MODEL PAPER 3

Listening

Item 1

1. (a) • She is 16
   • She is as old as Niklas
   (any one out of two) 1

   (b) • A cool outfit
   • A mini-skirt
   • A black T-shirt
   (any two out of three) 2

   (c) • Niklas took Helena home
   • The next weekend they went to the cinema together
   (any one out of two) 1

   (d) • She is never moody
   • She is patient
   • She is helpful
   • She is sporty
   • She is musical/interested in music
   (any two out of five) 2

   (e) • They want to travel through Europe
   • They want to go to London/Paris
   (any one out of two) 1

   (f)

Niklas cannot see himself staying with Helena.	
Niklas and Helena have a steady relationship.	✗
Niklas and Helena have no future plans.	

   1

Item 2

2. (a) She is 17 years old 1

   (b) • No time for a partner (at the moment)
   • Other things are more important
   • School is/school exams are more important
   • Hobbies are more important
   • Friends are more important
   (any two out of five) 2

   (c)

	True	False
Maria thinks that partners can share hobbies.		✗
Maria's sister has a boyfriend who likes football.	✗	
Maria's sister is interested in football.		✗

   3

   (d) • There is no such thing as a perfect partner
   • Nobody is perfect
   • Her ideal partner should make her laugh
   • Her ideal partner should have the same interests
   • Her ideal partner should be intelligent
   • Her ideal partner should have plans for the future
   • Her ideal partner should not smoke/be a non-smoker
   (any three out of seven) 3

   (e) • Trust
   • To help each other
   • To compromise 3

NATIONAL 5 GERMAN 2014

Reading

Text 1

(a) *Any two from:*
   • Work with a teacher in a small group
   • Discuss (their) work (with other pupils/teachers)
   • Develop/improve their talents/ideas

(b) *Any two from:*
   • You can plan (things) better
   • You have (much more) freedom
   • You learn to be independent

(c) (i) She was (a little) shy/she never said anything (in a normal class)

   (ii) • She has got to know (all pupils in) her group
   • She isn't afraid to give/state her opinion

(d) *Any two from:*
   • Appearance/the way you look/your look matters/is important
   • To keep/maintain/make (better) eye contact
   • To speak more slowly/more clearly

(e) Tick at **BOX 3**:
   Pupils who like working with others ✓

Text 2

(a) People/Humans going to the cinema/the number of cinema visitors/people going through/to the door(s)

(b) Any one from:
   • The (inter(national)) credit crunch/financial crisis/credit crisis/economic crisis
   • Many/(many) people have less/not enough/little money (at their disposal)

(c) • They have enough parking spaces (for everyone)/Plenty of parking
   • Tickets on special offer twice a week/2 days a week
   • A (10%) discount for regular visitors/regulars

(d) • (More and more) people have big(ger) screens/big(ger) screen TVs/big(ger) TVs
   • You can pause the film/it (when you want)
   • You can download/watch the latest/newest/new/(most) recent films/hits

(e) • Seven German films were made/appeared/opened (in 3D) last year
   • More than any country except the USA

Text 3

(a) Tick at **BOXES 2** and **3**:
   • Washing clothes
   • Showering

(b) • Well/fountain
   • River/burn

(c) • Dirty water/it leads to/carries (serious/bad) illness(es)/disease(s)/can make you sick/ill
   • (Can often be) fatal/deadly

(d) • (German) factories/industry use(s) a lot/quantities of chemicals/chemical products
   • The chemicals/they are (sometimes) poisonous/flow into the rivers (Please ensure that 'they' refers to a mention of chemicals in previous bullet point)

(e) *Any two from:*
- Water the plants/garden (no more than) once a week/(only) once a week
- Don't leave the tap running/Turn the tap off
- (Only) switch on/use the dishwasher when it is full

Writing

Please see the assessment criteria for Writing on pages 154–6.

NATIONAL 5 GERMAN 2014

Listening

Item 1

(a) Six months/half a year

(b) *Any one from:*
- (She works mostly) on the till/checkout/Scans the items (for customers)/(Works as) a cashier
- (She has to) fill/stack/refill/restock the <u>shelves</u> (every evening)

(c) (0)4.30 (pm)/16.30/half four

(d) (i) €6.50

(ii) (It is) well paid/(It's) good pay/(It is) good/a good amount

(e) *Any one from:*
- friendly
- helpful

(f) *Any one from:*
- She doesn't like it
- (It's) tiring
- (It's) (so/very) boring
- She has to sit for a long time

(g) Tick at **BOX 1**:
about how she works part-time and also manages to help out at home.

Item 2

(a) <u>Last</u>/<u>final</u> year

(b) 6.45 (am)/quarter to seven

(c) *Any one from:*
- (Go to) clubs/(school) orchestra
- Plays the <u>violin</u>

(d) That she <u>does/studies/learns/has/takes three</u> <u>foreign/</u><u>other</u> languages/French, Italian and English

(e) Ticks at **BOX 2** and **BOX 4**
- She is motivated in French.
- She works as well as she can.

(f) • She found it difficult/hard
- She couldn't concentrate (properly in the lesson)

(g) *Any two from:*
- Lara/She wasn't satisfied/happy/content at school
- She left school <u>at 16</u>/<u>this year</u>
- She has found a job at/in a vet's
- She is/enjoys working with animals (now)

(h) • (She hopes to do) a gap year/(She hopes to) go to/ visit/spend time in Australia or/and New Zealand (Both countries must be mentioned)
- (Her dream job would) be/work with children/ Be/work in a nursery/kindergarten/(primary) school/be a nursery teacher

NATIONAL 5 GERMAN 2015

Reading

Text 1

(a) *Accept any one of:* Shiver/quiver/tremble/shake/quake

(b) • Do not sit (at a desk) <u>for hours</u>
   • (Take) a break/pause <u>every 90 minutes/every hour and a half/after 90 minutes</u>

(c) *Any one from:*
   • Her <u>hands</u> sweat/she has sweaty <u>hands</u>
   • She loses her appetite/has no appetite/can't eat

(d) (i) (She practises/works on/does/goes over/prepares) it with a/her <u>friend</u>

   NB: insist on **friend (singular)**

   (ii) *Any one from:*
      • They do it in a new environment/surroundings/place
      • in a café <u>in town/in the city</u>
      • the <u>school</u> library

(e) • (Exam nerves are) normal/necessary

   (one adjective is sufficient)

   NB: Exam nerves are normal and necessary would only be awarded   **1 mark**

   • Without fear/worry you wouldn't take it/them seriously/Without stress, your exams would not come first

   NB: "Fear of exams is normal or you wouldn't take it seriously" should be awarded   **2 marks**

(f) (i) <u>Failing</u> (the exam) would be/is a <u>disaster/catastrophe</u>

   (ii) *Any one from:*
      • I (have) prepared/worked (for the exam)
      • I hope/aim/plan to get (a) good grade(s)/mark(s)/result(s)/I will do well

      NB: Insist on future intention

Text 2

(a) They paid <u>half</u> of her <u>travel/trip/journey</u> (costs)

(b) • Contact <u>between young people/teenagers in India and Germany</u>
   • Tolerance between <u>the</u> (two) <u>countries/between India and Germany/both lands</u>

(c) As a sign/symbol/gesture of friendship/to show friendship/to mark her friendship

(d) *Any three from:*
   • (Lots of) outings/trips/excursions
   • <u>Every evening/night/in the evening</u> there was a celebration/party/festival
   • There was Indian food <u>every evening/in the evening/for dinner</u>
   • A visit/trip/went to the parliament building (in New Delhi)

NB: Every evening they had a party with Indian food would be awarded **2 marks**. They had a party with Indian food would get **0 marks** because there is no indication of regularity.

(e) • Two pupils showed her books which <u>they</u> (had) read <u>in German</u>

   NB: It must be clear that the pupils read the books

   • Three boys told her about <u>two weeks</u> they spent in <u>Hamburg/Germany</u> (with a church group) **OR** time spent in <u>Hamburg/Germany with a church group</u>

   NB: It must be clear that the three boys spent time in Germany

(f) **BOX 2:** She wants to promote understanding between the two countries

Text 3

(a) **BOX 2:** Sara's work is not perfect but she is a good pupil

(b) *Any three from:*
   • It was (great) <u>fun</u>
   • It is creative <u>work</u>
   • You can work with/use your hands
   • You can experiment with/try out <u>new ideas</u>

(c) • It <u>tasted</u> great/it was tasty/yummy/tasteful
   • They sold it/you could buy it in <u>the confectioner's/in the (cake) shop/bakery</u>

(d) • (Sitting/Passing/Doing well in) exams
   • <u>Developing/discovering/finding</u> new talent(s) (one verb needed)

   NB: Accept "new talents to discover/develop" despite awkward word order

(e) *Any two from:*
   • It offers (an) insight(s) into/a view/experience of (the world of) work/You see/saw into/become familiar with (the world of) work
   • You can <u>learn from/through</u> (your own) experience
   • You can <u>make/get/gain</u> (personal) contact(s)

Writing

Please see the assessment criteria for Writing on pages 154–6.

NATIONAL 5 GERMAN 2015

Listening

Item 1

(a) 13th August

(b) Four years ago

OR

When he was 11 years old

(c) *Any two from:*
- (On) Wednesday(s)/every Wednesday
- Every second/other weekend
- Four weeks in the (school) holidays

(d) *Any two from:*
- (Spends) Christmas/it with his mother
- Visits/Sees/Stays with his dad two days later
- He gets two lots of/twice as many presents/presents from both parents

(e) He (always) gets good marks/grades/results

(f) **BOX 3:** He is positive

Item 2

(a) (Martin is Erik's) young(er)/little/small brother

(b) *Any one from:*
- They get on (quite) well

  OR
- He has a good relationship with his brother/It is good
- He can get on his nerves/he sometimes/now and again gets on his nerves/gets on his nerves when he comes into his room without knocking
- He likes him

(c) • Mother: Secretary/Works in an office (in town)

  NB: Secretary in a bureau is acceptable
- Father: Policeman/Police/Police officer

(d) His mum is allergic (to dogs)

  NB: Any recognisable spelling of "allergic" acceptable

(e) (i) Piano

   (ii) 3 years

(f) *Any three from:*
- He has three or four (really) good/close friends
- They are (quite) loud/noisy
- Fun/funny/a good laugh
- They have the same/similar interests

(g) *Any two from:*
- Go jogging in the (town) park
- Ride their bikes/go on bike rides/tours/cycle in the (local)area/neighbourhood
- Play in/for the school football team/Play football for the school
- Go to the cinema regularly
- Watch adventure films

Acknowledgements

Permission has been sought from all relevant copyright holders and Hodder Gibson is grateful for the use of the following:

Image © Rido/Fotolia (2014 Reading page 2);
Image © LifePhotoStudio/Shutterstock.com (2014 Reading page 4);
Image © Robin Heal/Shutterstock.com (2014 Reading page 6);
Image © wavebreakmedia/Shutterstock.com (2015 Reading page 2);
Image © OLJ Studio/Shutterstock.com (2015 Reading page 4);
Image © Pressmaster/Shutterstock.com (2015 Reading page 6).

Hodder Gibson would like to thank SQA for use of any past exam questions that may have been used in model papers, whether amended or in original form.